Green Line 5

2. Fremdsprache

Workbook

von
Jennifer Baer-Engel
Geraldine Greenhalgh
Melissa Keller
Jon Marks
Dr. Karoline Wellner
Alison Wooder

Ernst Klett Verlag
Stuttgart · Leipzig

Workbook Audios / Filme

Track	Chapter	Page	Ex.	Time	Title
A1–2	Across cultures 1	3	2	10:14	A podcast on respect
V1	Focus 1	4	1	7:13	Scotland's ancient past
A3	Unit 1	10	6	6:36	A Scottish stand-up comedy show
A4	Unit 1	11	8	9:40	The Glasgow Mural Trail
V2	Unit 1	17	14	6:24	Going downhill
A5–6	Unit 1	18	16	10:25	The cattle of Pabbay
V3	Unit 1	19	17	5:51	The forgotten island of Belnahua
A7–8	Focus 3	27	2	9:49	Harriet Tubman – runaway, conductor and spy
A9–10	Unit 2	32	5	11:39	The Nickel – from zydeco music to football saints
A11–12	Unit 2	33	7	9:18	Black History Month
V4	Unit 2	35	10	9:29	Black People Made That!
A13–15	Unit 3	51	3	11:57	Talking about generations
V5	Unit 3	54	8	4:19	Hip hop in education
A16	Unit 3	63	20	10:17	Female fandom
A17	Unit 3	64	22	7:37	Fashion in subcultures

Schulbuch Audios

Track	Chapter	Page	Ex.	Time	Title
A1	Unit 1	13	4	1:56	The Scottish Prince
A2	Unit 1	14	1	3:34	Leaving city life behind
A3–9	Unit 1	16	4	7:15	The lonely campsite
A10–11	Unit 1	18	5	2:59	Daniel's perspective
A12	Unit 1	20	1	2:21	Glasgow's miles better than this portrayal of a hopeless, ...
A13	Unit 1	22	3	3:25	The Edinburgh Fringe Festival
A14–21	Unit 1	29	1	16:38	Taming the kelpie
A22	Focus 2	32	3a)	0:49	To a Mouse
A23–24	Focus 3	38	5	4:13	The great emancipator?
A25–30	Unit 2	42	1	10:45	Living in two worlds
A31	Unit 2	46	4	3:44	School experiences
A32	Unit 2	47	5	1:48	The Heart of Harlem
A33–38	Unit 2	48	1	6:01	Five things to know about black culture now
A39	Unit 2	51	1	1:47	Why Kamala Harris and 'Firsts' Matter
A40–42	Unit 2	52	2	5:36	Barack Obama – yes, he tried?
A43–47	Unit 2	57	1	9:32	On the come up
A48–53	Unit 3	70	1	10:42	Two worlds colliding
A54–59	Unit 3	73	2	10:00	The importance of music
A60	Unit 3	76	2	3:11	Artist, Icon, Billionaire: How Jay-Z created his $1 billion fortune
A61	Unit 3	80	3	3:35	Teenage girls show the scary effects of editing apps
A62–66	Unit 3	81	4	7:43	Youth subcultures: what are they now?
A67	Unit 3	85	1	0:39	The rose that grew from concrete
A68	Unit 3	85	1	1:27	And 2Morrow
A69	Unit 3	86	1	3:48	Role models?
A70	Unit 3	87	1	4:30	Pushing buttons: Gaming is culture
A71–77	Extra Line	100	–	15:38	Secrets
A78	Extra Line	104	–	1:19	I'm Rooting for Everybody Black
A79	Extra Line	104	–	0:41	I, too
A80	Extra Line	104	–	1:04	Malcolm X, February 1965
A81	Extra Line	105	–	2:31	Dear Basketball
A82–84	Extra Line	106	–	9:00	Two unlikely friends
A85	Text smart	108	2	1:09	The Look
A86	Text smart	109	3	1:44	War photographer
A87	Text smart	109	4	1:38	The words of poems
A88	Text smart	110	2	3:25	Mary Queen of Scots Got Her Head Chopped Off

VOCABULARY

1 Two perspectives on being different → SB 8/3

Complete Jonathan's and Bisra's personal accounts with the correct forms of these words.

accessible | to adapt | to be discriminated against | ethnic | to face many difficulties | inappropriate | inclusion | to live with a disability | to make a judgement | multicultural | to not experience discrimination | open-minded | stereotype | uncomfortable | to use a wheelchair | to wear a hijab

Jonathan I didn't realise the importance of ________________ until I had ________________ myself. After my accident, my family and I ________________ such as moving to an ________________ home and getting used to ________________ ________________. In the beginning, I felt ________________ with answering so many questions about my disability, but my nurse told me that people only wanted to understand what had happened. I realised that it also took the people around me time ________________!

Bisra Luckily, New York's population is diverse and ________________. People here are ________________ and don't care what ________________ background you come from, so I ________________ ________________ in my daily life often and I rarely get any ________________ comments. But like many other women who ________________, I ________________. Sometimes it's everyday questions like "Are you forced to cover your hair?" which remind me that people ________________ based on ________________.

LISTENING

2 A podcast on respect → SB 9/5; S13, S16

A1–2

a) *For a school project in ethics you have to give a presentation on the topic "Respekt". Your teacher gave you the link to a helpful podcast in English in which the expert Dr Langman talks about respect. Listen to the podcast and take notes.*

MEDIATION

b) *To prepare for your presentation you have met up with a partner. Explain to each other in German what you understood about the different forms of respect and disrespect and discuss which examples you want to include in your presentation.*

SPEAKING

c) *Part of the school project is to make your school a more respectful place. With your partner, discuss three things you could implement to make everyone feel more accepted and respected.*

Focus 1 Scottish history

VIEWING

1 Scotland's ancient past → SB 10/1; S19

V1

a) *Watch this video in which a reporter interviews Chris, a loch-diver, and visits an Iron Age[1] festival. Complete the definition.*

A crannog is an ancient ________________ ________________ constructed in a ________________.

b) *Explain why the ceramics that Chris found in a loch on the Hebrides changed Scottish history.*

____

____

____

c) *Answer these questions.*

1. What can you find inside a crannog? (four things) ____

____

2. How long did it take to build a crannog during the Iron Age? ________________________

3. What were the three main reasons why crannogs were built on water? ________________

____

VOCABULARY

2 Scotland and England → SB 11/3

a) *Complete the text about the history between Scotland and England. Use synonyms (=), opposites (↔) or other related words (→) for the words in blue.*

During the war for Scottish independence from England, Scottish warriors ________________ (= to win against) English soldiers in several ________________ (→ to rebel), unforgettably for Scottish history in the Battle of Bannockburn in 1314. In spite of being recognised as an ________________ (= separate) country in 1328, the conflict between Scotland and England did not ____________ (↔ to begin). In the 16th century, the Scottish parliament ________________ (↔ to allow) the English prince to ____________ (↔ to divorce) Mary I of Scotland, so that Scotland would still be ________________ (→ reign) independently. This upset the English king so much that he sent the English ________________ (= military) to ________________ (→ invasion) Scotland.

1 Iron Age ['aɪən ˌeɪdʒ] Eisenzeit

Mary ____________ (= to get away from danger) to France, a political partner against England, where she married a French prince and ____________ (= to stay) until his ____________ (→ dead). Returning to a Protestant country after the Scottish Reformation, Queen Elizabeth I of England saw Mary, a Catholic, as a threat to ____________ (↔ war) in the country. That's why Mary was ____________ (= to be made to do) to give up her power, and her baby son became King James VI of Scotland. In 1603 Elizabeth I of England ____________ (→ dead) without children, so James VI inherited the English throne, becoming James I of England. This Union of the Crowns brought the two countries much closer ____________ (↔ apart). Finally, in 1707 ____________ (= England, Scotland and Wales) was created.

b) *In your exercise book, use the words from the text to create a mind map with thematic vocabulary on* ***monarchy***, ***war*** *and* ***church****. Add your own ideas.*

READING

3 The Queen of Edinburgh society

→ SB 11/4; S5–6

a) *Read the article about Alison Cockburn, who brought together the great minds of the Scottish Enlightenment, and complete the exercises in your exercise book.*

Alison Cockburn (born Alison Rutherford in 1712) was a Scottish songwriter, poet and humorous writer who had many famous friends of the Enlightenment age. These included novelist Walter Scott, economist Adam Smith, philosopher David Hume and Scotland's most famous poet, Robert Burns. She became known as the 'Queen' of Edinburgh society.

In 1731, Alison married a lawyer named Patrick Cockburn. They did not have a lot of money and for four years they had to live with his father, who was very religious and disapproved of socialising. When her father-in-law died, Alison and her husband moved to Edinburgh. Alison's lively personality and humour soon made her popular with the city's wealthy elite, even though she herself was not wealthy.

After her husband died in 1753, Alison continued to have a busy social life, and her home became a centre for artists and intellectuals from Scotland and further away to meet and exchange ideas. She had begun to write before her husband's death, and in 1745 she was very nearly arrested for writing a humorous piece which criticised a member of the royal family. Her most famous work is a set of song lyrics called *Flowers of the Forest*, which was published in 1765.

Alison Cockburn died in 1794 aged 72. She was unusual perhaps not so much for what she did as the fact that she did it as a woman. At the time, it was very unusual for a woman to be so active in this way – especially a woman whose husband was dead – and many people disapproved of her. However, it seems that this did not worry her, and the famous artists and intellectuals who were her friends clearly valued her friendship and respected her as an equal.

b) *Create a time line of Alison Cockburn's life.*

c) *Describe Alison Cockburn's personality and explain her role in the Scottish Enlightenment (100 words).*

Unit 1 Scotland

VOCABULARY

1 Why you should visit Scotland → SB 13/4

a) *Complete this website about Scotland's attractions with the correct forms of these words. Add prepositions where necessary.*

ancient | to appear | castle | famous | to focus | geography | Highlands | landscape | loch | to manufacture | to offer | ride | space | tradition | to travel | view | work

There are a lot of well-known reasons to love Scotland – the beautiful mountains of the Scottish ________________, the mystic ________________ and ________________ cities with their centuries-old ________________ – but Scotland has even more ________________.

A ________________ the Harry Potter train: The Glenfinnan Viaduct ________________ many films and TV shows, but most ________________ in the shots of the Hogwarts Express in the Harry Potter movies. On the Jacobite Steam Train tourists ________________ a route which includes the viaduct and fantastic ________________ the wild Scottish ________________.

The Scottish Space Age: Sure, Scotland celebrates its ________________, but it's also firmly ________________ the future. Glasgow ________________ more satellites than any other European city, and more than 130 companies ________________ Scotland's space industry. In fact, the Highlands and Islands have ideal ________________ for sending rockets[1] ________________.

b) *As an intern at the tourist information centre you have to write two more paragraphs (each about 60 words) on "Why you should visit Scotland". Use these ideas or your own and research online.*

street food | festivals | bothies | renewable energy | literature | golf | tartan

WRITING

2 Typically Scottish? → SB 13/4; S4, S17

a) *Write a short text (about 120 words) about the cartoon. Follow these steps:*

1. Describe the cartoon.
2. Compare the stereotypes used to portray Scottish and English people.

b) *With your partner, discuss portraying nationalities using stereotypes. Talk about where stereotypes about nationalities come from and which purpose they can have in different contexts (e.g. cartoons, advertisements).*

1 rocket ['rɒkɪt] Rakete

MEDIATION

3 Moving to a remote[1] Scottish island → SB 14/1; S16

a) *Your friend Penelope, who lives in London, is fascinated by the idea to move to a Scottish island. Use this article and write an English e-mail to her (about 180 words) in which you explain the problems that the islands and their inhabitants are facing, why that is the case and which solutions the government is planning.*

Schottland will 60.000 Euro verschenken – ihr müsst nur auf diese Inseln ziehen

Das Leben auf einer abgeschotteten Insel ist für viele ein Lebenstraum. Dennoch kämpfen die schottischen Nordseeinseln mit einem Bevölkerungsschwund. Das soll sich jetzt ändern.

Mit einem millionenschweren Konjunkturprogramm will das Parlament in Edinburgh dafür sorgen, dass es mehr Menschen auf die bislang eher verlassenen schottischen Inseln im Atlantik und der Nordsee zieht.

Vieles spricht dagegen, dort zu leben: Eine schlechte Infrastruktur, raues Klima, kalte Winter. Doch rund 50.000 Pfund, umgerechnet sind das in etwa 58.687 Euro, sollen überzeugen. So viel Geld sollen die ersten 100 Menschen unter 30 Jahren beziehungsweise Familien bekommen, die es auf eine der ausgewählten schottischen Inseln zieht. Die Finanzspritze hat die Region auch bitter nötig: Die Bewohner der Insel werden immer älter. Viele ziehen lieber in die schottischen Städte wie Glasgow, Edinburgh, Dundee oder eben gleich in die britische Hauptstadt London.

Umzugswillige, die von dem Inselbonus profitieren wollen, müssen eine der folgenden Bezirke und deren Inseln zu ihrem neuen Hauptwohnort erklären sowie dort ihren Lebensmittelpunkt haben: Argyll, Arran, Bute, Great Cumbrae, die Äußeren Hebriden mit den Inseln Lewis and Harris sowie Uist und Barra, das Orkney-Archipel, die Shetlandinseln oder die Insel Skye sowie die benachbarten Small Isles. Mithilfe der Fördergelder soll den Neu-Insulanern der Start in der neuen Heimat etwas angenehmer gemacht werden, wie die britische BBC berichtet.

Einige Inselbewohner befürchten nun, dass es einen Wettbewerb unter den Inselkommunen geben wird, wer mehr neue Einwohner für sich gewinnen kann, wie Iain Stephen Morrison, Journalist, gegenüber der BBC erklärt. Seiner Meinung nach könnten die insgesamt fünf Millionen Pfund besser investiert werden. Etwa in den Ausbau der Infrastruktur, was die Inseln auf lange Sicht attraktiver machen würde: „Es mangelt nicht an Menschen, die auf die Insel ziehen wollen. Was fehlt sind Chancen – sei es Wohnraum oder Arbeitsplätze."

Dass einige Schotten sich durchaus vorstellen können, auf eine der Inseln im Atlantik oder der Nordsee zu leben, die Hürden aber groß sind, zeigt das Beispiel von Kevin Morrison. Laut einem BBC-Bericht ist er vor gut fünf Jahren von Glasgow nach Uist an der schottischen Westküste gezogen – und hätte die Starthilfe gut gebrauchen können.

„Das wäre damals sicher praktisch gewesen. Die Hauptthemen für Inselgemeinden sind der Transport von und zu den Inseln sowie das Wohnen", so Kevin Morrison. Sie hätten damals voll auf Risiko gesetzt: Seine Frau, die aus Uist kommt, und er hätten ihre sicheren Vollzeitjobs in Glasgow aufgegeben und gegen das Leben auf dem Eiland getauscht.

Ab dem kommenden Jahr sollen anderen Menschen, die sich wie Morrison und seine Frau entscheiden, auf eine der schottischen Inseln zu ziehen, etwas mehr finanzielle Sicherheit haben. Ob die Pläne tatsächlich umgesetzt werden, darüber muss bis zum 24. Oktober noch das schottische Parlament abstimmen. Bis 2025 wollen die Politikerinnen und Politiker in Edinburgh alles daran setzen, dass die gälische Kultur der zum Teil abgelegenen Gebiete weiter gestärkt wird. Auf der Insel Argyll leben zurzeit etwa 130 Menschen, nur 30 davon sind jünger als 50 Jahre alt. Die Grundschule der Insel besuchen aktuell nur vier Kinder. Alarmierende Zahlen also.

Um einen weiteren Bevölkerungsschwund zu vermeiden, sollen neben der finanziellen Förderung von Zugezogenen auch der Ausbau nachhaltiger Energien und des öffentlichen Nahverkehrs auf den Inseln verbessert werden. Auch Projekte zur Förderung der mentalen Gesundheit sollen unterstützt werden.

Sabine Winkler, Welt, 2021 (adaptiert)

SPEAKING

b) *Discuss with a partner why you would (not) move to a remote Scottish island.*

1 remote [rɪˈməʊt] abgelegen

SPEAKING

4 Living in remote[1] rural Scotland → SB 14/1; S18

a) *Look at these statistics comparing life in different places in Scotland. Talk about the results with a partner. How does living in a remote rural area influence the life of teenagers? What advantages and disadvantages are there?*

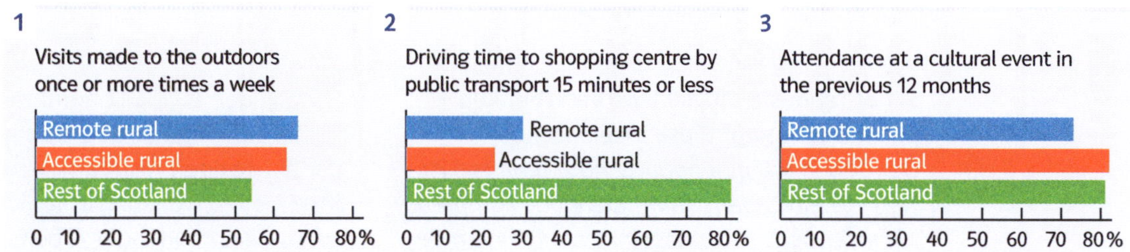

Source: Cabinet Secretary of Rural Affairs and Islands, 2021

b) *Do a survey in class on the aspects from a) and compare your results to the statistics of Scotland.*

READING

5 Scotland's most famous monster → SB 15/2; S5–7

a) *Read the article and do the exercises on the following page.*

Scientists to lead DNA hunt for Loch Ness monster

Samples[2] of the Scottish loch will be tested to reveal truth behind centuries-old legend

An examination of Loch Ness using DNA sampling techniques will try to establish exactly what lives in the UK's largest freshwater[3] body[4] by volume – it may also discover whether there is any scientific basis to the monster legend.

The mission will involve genetic code being extracted from the loch over a two-week period to determine the types of creatures that live there.

Prof Neil Gemmell, a scientist from New Zealand leading the global team of researchers, said: "I'm going into this thinking it's unlikely there is a monster, but I want to test that hypothesis. What we'll get is a really nice survey of the biodiversity of Loch Ness."

After the team's trip next month, the samples will be sent to labs in Australia, Denmark, France and New Zealand to be analysed.

"There's absolutely no doubt that we will find new stuff, and that's very exciting," Gemmell said. "While the possibility of looking for proof of the Loch Ness monster is the hook to this project, there is an exceptional amount of new knowledge that we will gain from the work about organisms that inhabit Loch Ness."

Many believe sightings of the "monster" could in fact be a large fish, such as a catfish[5] or sturgeon[6]. Scientists will explore this theory during their investigation.

Whenever a creature moves through its environment, it leaves tiny fragments of DNA from skin, scales, feathers, fur, faeces[7] and urine.

Gemmell said: "This DNA can be captured, sequenced and then used to identify that creature by comparing the sequence found to large databases of known genetic sequences from hundreds of thousands of different organisms."

He predicts they will document new species of life, particularly bacteria, and provide important data on the number of several new invasive species recently seen in the loch, such as Pacific pink salmon.

Adrian Shine, a local expert and lead researcher on the Loch Ness Project will also join the team.

There was a wave of excitement among Nessie hunters in 2016 when sonar images revealed something at the bottom of the loch

1 remote [rɪˈməʊt] abgelegen ○ **2** sample [ˈsɑːmpl] Probe ○ **3** freshwater [ˈfreʃˌwɔːtə] Süßwasser ○ **4** body [ˈbɒdi] Gewässer ○ **5** catfish [ˈkætfɪʃ] Wels ○ **6** sturgeon [ˈstɜːdʒn] Stör ○ **7** faeces *(pl)* [ˈfiːsiːz] Exkremente that looked like the shape commonly assigned to the beast.

It turned out, however, that Shine and his team had discovered an abandoned prop from the 1970 film *The Private Life of Sherlock Holmes*. The 10-metre (30ft) model was discovered 180 metres beneath the surface by a robot, which was examining the loch.

Stories about the loch hiding a monster date to the seventh century. Adomnán's *Life of St Columba* tells of the saint encountering "a water beast". Columba is reported to have saved a man from the creature by ordering it to go away. In modern times, more than 1,000 people have claimed to have seen Nessie, which has in turn benefitted the local tourist industry. The nearby village of Drumnadrochit is home to two permanent Loch Ness monster displays.

The development of photography caused wider interest in the legend, and photographs taken in 1933 and 1934 featured on the front pages of national newspapers.

The 1934 image, known as 'the surgeon's photograph', which appears to show a creature with a long neck and head coming out of the water, is probably the most famous picture of the monster.

It was revealed as a hoax in 1994 by Christian Spurling, who said his stepfather, Marmaduke Wetherell, had arranged the stunt with the photographer Col Robert Wilson. The "creature" in the picture was in fact a toy submarine with a fake snake head.

In 2003, the BBC funded a search that used 600 sonar beams and satellite tracking to examine the loch. The team had speculated that a plesiosaur, a species that became extinct with the dinosaurs, may have survived in the cool loch, despite the preference of marine reptiles for subtropical waters. However, their search showed there was no hint of such a creature.

Martin Belam, The Guardian, 2018 (adapted)

b) *Look at these words in the text and match them with the correct pictures.*

3 scales (l. 37) 1 sonar (l. 53, l. 90) 4 saint (l. 65) 2 submarine (l. 87)

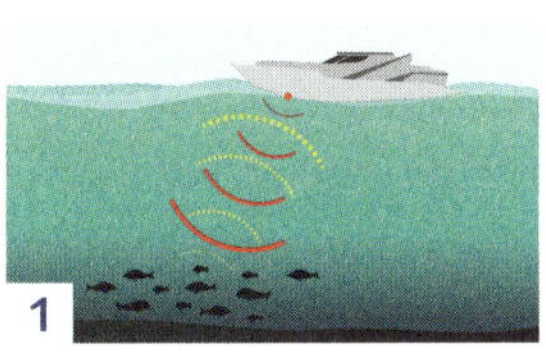
1

2

3

4

c) *Name the different theories given in the article on what the Loch Ness monster could be.*

d) *Copy and complete this grid about the research on Loch Ness in your exercise book.*

year	method of research	(expected) outcome
2018	…	…

e) *Are these statements true, false or not in the text? Tick the correct answer.*

	true	false	not in the text
1. The Loch Ness monster is beneficial for the tourism in the region.	X		
2. Thanks to the widespread accessibility of photography, more and more people have been able to provide proof of Nessie sightings.			X
3. To this day the 'surgeon's photograph' is one of the most reliable shots of Nessie.	X		

f) *In your exercise book, analyse the use of quotes in the text.*

WRITING

g) *Research online and write a short informative text (about 60 words) which could be featured alongside the article on one of these topics:*

DNA sequencing St Columba where the 'surgeon's photograph' got its name from

LISTENING

6 A Scottish stand-up comedy show → SB 19/6; S13

A3

a) *Listen to this stand-up comedy show about Scottish stereotypes and tick ✔ the topics the comedian talks about.*

1. ☐ weather
2. ☐ Scottish people being extraordinarily friendly
3. ☐ tartan
4. ☐ clans
5. ☐ bagpipes
6. ☐ shortbread
7. ☐ Loch Ness Monster
8. ☐ rivalry between England and Scotland

b) *Listen again and tick ✔ the statements / jokes the comedian makes.*

1. ☐ English people think the Scottish smile too much.
2. ☐ Especially cartoons use the stereotype of Scots wearing tartan.
3. ☐ The comedian wears a kilt to show off to tourists.
4. ☐ Tartan clothing shouldn't be sold as a souvenir.
5. ☐ Bagpipe tunes[1] sound very similar.
6. ☐ Bagpipe players should only be allowed to play the bagpipes outside.

c) *Complete the sentence.*

Shortbread is made from flour[2], ____________________ and baked ____________________.

d) *Answer these questions in your exercise book. Take notes.*

1. According to the comedian, why is it so funny that Scottish shortbread is sold all around the world?
2. How does the comedian use irony to describe the historic relationship between England and Scotland?

LANGUAGE

7 Find the mistakes: Highland Games → SB 19/6

Read this internet review of a Highland games event written by a German visitor. Decide if the underlined phrases are correct or not. Correct the mistakes.

While (1) visited Scotland with my family, we (2) were seeing a poster for 'Highland games'. So, we decided (3) going even though we didn't know (4) what to expect. The 'games' were all very traditional. There was (5) 'tug o'war', which involves two teams pulling on a rope and (6) try pulling the other team (7) above a line, 'caber toss' (throwing a tree pole), hammer throw … The event (8) all day lasted and there were (9) foods stands, stalls selling local crafts, activities for children, music (including (10) the bagpipe music) and dancing. To be honest, I found the (11) actual games a little boring. It (12) quite was interesting (13) to watch the first two or three people throw a big tree pole, but then I felt that I (14) had had enough. However, there was (15) very good atmosphere and it really didn't seem a thing that (16) had put on for tourists. It was a local event for local people. In some Scottish places, if you (17) saw people wearing tartan and doing Scottish dancing, it (18) maybe to entertain tourists. In this case, though, I felt I was seeing (and hearing!) (19) the 'real' Scotland. It was perhaps (20) the better day of our holiday and I (21) do recommend (22) to see a Highland games event if you (23) will ever get the chance.

____
____
____
____
____
____
____
____
____
____
____

1 tune [tjuːn] Melodie 2 flour [flaʊə] Mehl

LISTENING

8 The Glasgow Mural[1] Trail → SB 20/1; S13

A4

a) *Listen to this radio programme in which a reporter presents the Glasgow Mural Trail. Tick ✔ the murals that are mentioned and match them with the artists that created them. There's one extra.*

Cobolt | Molly Hankinson | Rogue One | Smug

1 ☐ ____________ 2 ☐ ____________ 3 ☐ ____________ 4 ☐ ____________ 5 ☐ ____________

b) *Listen to part 1 and complete the text.*

The Glasgow Mural Trail is a tour through Glasgow which includes ____________ of the city's best graffiti artworks In ____________, the city council[2] decided to officially implement graffiti works of art into the urban space in order to ____ __________ and to ____.

Their plan worked out and the artworks became popular with ______________ and ______________.

c) *Are these statements true or false? Tick ✔ the correct answer.*

	true	false
1. Saint Mungo is the patron saint[3] of Glasgow.	☐	☐
2. According to legend, Saint Mungo brought a bird back to life.	☐	☐
3. Smug's artworks are known for being abstract.	☐	☐

d) *Listen to part 2 and take notes on the different opinions on the Glasgow Mural Trail.*

who	opinion
reporter	
American visitor	
Glasgow native	

WRITING

e) *Write a letter (about 150 words) to a representative of the local government of your town/city. Explain why it would be a good idea to have a street art project like Glasgow's.*

1 mural ['mjʊərl] Wandmalerei ○ 2 city council [ˌsɪti 'kaʊnsl] Stadtrat ○ 3 patron saint [ˌpeɪtrn 'seɪnt] Schutzpatron/-in

LANGUAGE

9 Mixed bag: Oil, football and butteries → SB 21/2

Complete this blog entry a student posted online about his hometown Aberdeen.

Some people ___ think there ___ only two important cities in Scotland: Glasgow ___ Edinburgh, but ___ is wrong! Scotland ___ several amazing cities, ___ with its ___ identity and things ___ it special. Aberdeen is ___ third ___ city in Scotland and is home ___ Aberdeen Harbour – a very important port for the oil and gas industry. ___, Aberdeen ___ (often) the oil capital of Europe, ___ of course we hope ___ a few years from now because oil ___ by renewable energies. The Aberdeen Football Club is ___ of the best in Scotland. And not ___ do we have a great team, ___ we have a fantastic stadium too. The Pittodrie Stadium holds 20,000 people, ___ is about 10 % of Aberdeen's population. In addition to that, the city is famous for ___ buttery, which is ___ kind of flat bread roll we Aberdonians ___ for breakfast. I ___ to eat butteries a lot. I ___ have one for breakfast almost ___ day until I ___ out how ___ fat and sugar ___ in them. ___ to Aberdeen, you shouldn't miss out on ___ one though!

READING

10 All of the above → SB 22/3; S5–6, S10–11

a) *Anna, after losing her father and being bullied online, and her mother move from Birmingham to the small Scottish village of St Monans for a fresh start. Even though she has made some friends at her new school, Anna is worried that eventually people will find out about her past. Read the novel excerpt and do the exercises.*

As I walk through the main entrance of St Margaret's, a weird quiet seems to follow me. Whispers die as I come closer and spring back to life again in my wake[1]. Eyeballs are everywhere. Their gaze[2] crawls all over me like a thousand spiders. I try not to scratch myself. Am I imagining it? Is that cluster of older girls looking me up and down or are they focusing on the noticeboard behind me? "It's not all about you, Anna," I whisper under my breath, desperately trying to calm myself. "Jeez, you only just got here – most people don't even know who you are yet." A group of boys I don't know are laughing as I turn a corner. When they see me, they seem to laugh louder, or am I just being paranoid? As I step into the art block for the first lesson, I feel the anxiety[3] loosen its grip on my chest just a little. Neither Alisha nor Cat is in the same art class as me so I settle down at a workbench on my own. Within fifteen minutes, I've decided that I've definitely been imagining the whole thing.

After art class, Anna walks to her next lesson.

Rounding a corner, I find my path blocked by a group of boys I don't know. But, as I try to walk

1 in sb's wake [weɪk] im Gefolge ○ **2** gaze [geɪz] Blick ○ **3** anxiety [æŋˈzaɪəti] Sorge past, one of them purposely steps in front of me, blocking my way. I move to walk round him and he sidesteps, trapping me between him and the lockers. "Hey, Anna," he sings in a teasing voice, "fancy a threesome[1]?" Some of the others laugh rowdily. I try to push past him, but he moves sideways again, backing me against a locker door. "C'mon," he croons, "don't be like that. I know you want it … I've seen your Facebook page." He moves closer, his breath hot on my face. "Isn't this what you like, Anna Clark?" And then his voice drops to a whisper. "Or should I say Anna Reeves?" A shock runs through my body like electricity. I dive sideways and escape, running down the corridor. I hear laughter and shouts behind me. How does he know that name?

I stumble through the main door as the bell rings for the next period. I don't walk far. I can't. I have to see it. I have to know. I stumble down a few streets, far enough away from school to avoid the risk of being spotted, until I reach a small, treelined square. I sink down against the trunk of a tree and pull out my phone. I google "Anna Reeves Facebook", and find what I'm looking for almost immediately. Someone has set up a new profile and it's not exactly easy to miss. I can't log in, but I don't need an account to view it – the profile is public. Of course it is. As public as possible. How did I ever think I could outrun this?

The main profile picture is an old one of me, cropped from a photo on someone else's account. I'm at a party and the side of someone else's smiling face is still just visible next to mine. Under "work and education" it says: "Founder of Sluts[2] United". And then, underneath, there it is. The picture I've been running away from, the feeling I literally left the country to escape, the shame that's been trying to get back inside my mind ever since we got here. The photograph I've tried over and over to forget, the one I've deleted all copies and evidence[3] of. And yet here it is again, turned against me like a weapon. I feel sick and close my eyes. My blood is rushing loud in my ears. Everything else is quiet. I click and zoom and examine it, as if looking for long enough might dissolve it, dissolve me. I look until my own skin very slowly starts to blur and collapse in on itself through my tears.

Over fifty people are listed as friends – Simon Stewart … Charlie Eppingham … Louise Campbell – I can see their grinning faces in the list at the side of the page. Whoever created the profile must have searched for St Margaret's and it looks like they've added practically everyone in our year. Some are people I've slowly started making friends with; some I've barely even met. Well, they all know me now.

Panicking, I tap hard at the picture with my finger, desperate to delete it, to make it disappear. But, without my own account, there's no way of accessing it. My fingers fly over the screen. I create a new profile, entering the bare minimum of information, using my old hotmail address and not bothering to fill in any personal information or add a picture. As soon as I'm in, I return to the Anna Reeves page and click again on the photo, looking for the report button. The first option is simple enough. "I'm in this photo and I don't like it." Click. Then a new set of options fills the screen. I hesitate.

- It's a bad photo of me
- It's inappropriate
- It makes me sad
- It's embarrassing
- Other

Where's "All of the above" when you need it? Finally, I jab at "It's inappropriate". "The best way to remove this photo is to ask Anna to take it down," Facebook chirps helpfully. "Message Anna to resolve this?" "Yeah, right," I mumble. I've tried that before. After everything I've been through, after all the lengths we went to to get away, I'm right back where I started. How could this have happened? I've been so careful. How did he know where I am, the name of my new school? It doesn't make any sense. How did he find me? It's a strange combination, anger and shame. It feels like acid[4] burning in your veins[5]. I open a new message window on my phone and type in a number I know by heart. Then I write this message:

Please. Just leave me alone.

And I hit send.

From: Laura Bates, *The Burning* (adapted)

1 threesome *(infml)* ['θriːsəm] Dreier *(ugs.)* ○ 2 slut [slʌt] *Schimpfwort für Frauen* ○ 3 evidence ['evɪdns] Beweismaterial ○ 4 acid ['æsɪd] Säure ○ 5 vein [veɪn] Vene

b) *Use the context to guess the meaning of these words and match them with the definitions.*

1. to loosen one's grip (l. 18)
2. to fancy (l. 30)
3. to croon (l. 33)
4. to dissolve (l. 72)
5. to blur (l. 73)
6. to chirp (l. 105)

a) to become difficult to see clearly
b) to disappear
c) to hold sth less tightly
d) to say sth in a happy way
e) to talk in a low and soft voice
f) to want

c) *Bring the events in the order in which they happen. There's one extra statement.*

- ☐ Anna is bullied by a boy.
- ☐ Anna checks social media.
- ☐ Anna is at a party.
- ☐ Anna goes to her art class.
- ☐ Anna sends a text message.
- ☐ Anna cries over a picture of her online.

d) *Answer these questions. Take notes.*

1. How does Anna feel when she walks into school that morning? ____________________

____

2. Why is Anna shocked when the boy calls her Anna Reeves? ____________________

____

e) *Are these statements true or false? Tick ✔ the correct answer and correct the wrong statements.*

	true	false
1. The fake social media profile of Anna Reeves is private. Correction: ____________________		
2. On the friend list are over fifty people from Anna's old school. Correction: ____________________		
3. Anna sets up an account to report the picture. Correction: ____________________		
4. The solution that Facebook offers is helpful. Correction: ____________________		

f) *In your exercise book, analyse how the author creates suspense. Think about: the information (not) given, the narrative perspective and style.*

g) *Discuss these questions with a partner.*

1. What could be the reasons why Anna changed her name?
2. What could be in the picture of Anna that was posted online?
3. Who could be the person whom Anna sends the text message to?

WRITING

h) *Choose **one** of the following tasks. Write about 150 words in your exercise book.*

1. In the introduction of the book Anna compares rumours to fire. Comment on this comparison.
2. Anna tells her friends Cat and Alisha that she is being bullied and asks them for advice. Write a scene, including dialogue and stage directions and act it out.

READING **11** **Cool, confident and Scottish** → SB 23/1; S4–6

a) *Read the article about Scotland's hip-hop scene and do the exercises in your exercise book.*

'It was like: people from Aberdeen shouldn't rap!' Scotland's hidden hip-hop scene

At Hang, Scotland's first hip-hop conference, the country's MCs are given a hero's welcome – but there's also important discussion about the prejudices they face.

"Here's a golden oldie," Nova laughs, breaking into her 2019 single 3am. The crowd scream like she's just won Olympic gold. This is Hang – Scotland's first hip-hop conference – and it's the Edinburgh rapper's first live show since she bagged the Scottish Album of the Year award in 2020 for her debut Re-Up. Topping off a day packed with DJ workshops, breakdance, spoken word and panels of industry experts, Nova's triumphant headline set is a middle finger to anyone who still thinks there's no hip-hop in Scotland.

Ransom FA, an Aberdonian rapper who's shared stages with heavyweights such as Skepta and Wiley, says: "One of the biggest hurdles I had was being a young Black kid with a Scottish accent trying to enter an English-based scene. It was like: people from Aberdeen shouldn't rap!" He raises an eyebrow questioningly. Edinburgh MC Lotos shares a similar story: "When I first started out, people didn't see it as viable to be a Scottish rapper. I'd come to London and they'd be like, 'They've got Black people in Scotland?'"

Created by the Scottish Alternative Music Awards (Sama) in partnership with Creative Scotland, Hang (Hip-hop Aimed Networking with Grime) is designed to give a career boost to artists working to overturn these roadblocks. For the charismatic, genre-hopping young rapper Chef, the night doubled as a release party – his new EP The World Is Mine dropped at midnight – and he's coolly confident that Hang is one more sign that the Scottish scene is set to explode. "In five, 10 years we'll be looking back on tonight," he grins. "We'll be saying: that's when I met that artist, that's where I made those connections. For us to be able to get together and share our knowledge, it's really very important."

Despite those persistent assumptions that Scotland isn't home to hip-hop, its music and culture has been central to the Scottish cultural underground ever since it first crossed the Atlantic. Hip-hop's energy, artistry, community spirit and political expression made a major impact on young Scots in the 80s, inspiring them to speak up about social injustice. Homegrown hip-hop records followed in the early 90s, when Scottish rappers began to embrace their own accents while remaining inspired by the sounds and attitudes that began in the Bronx. Many of those early key players are at Hang, sharing their experiences with a new generation of passionate artists.

Where London-centric English rap is increasingly collaborative around the country, the Scottish scene has always been this way. Chef's new EP is a tour through Scotland's cities, recorded with rising stars in Aberdeen, Dundee, Glasgow and Edinburgh. "There's a massive difference between Scottish and English rap," he says, "and I think those differences should be celebrated. The English have their own sound already, and I'm obviously inspired by London grime, but Scottish artists are striving to make international sounds." His goal? "We're going to be worldwide. I know it."

Katie Hawthrone, The Guardian, 2021 (adapted)

b) *Make a list of unknown words and phrases from the text. Which of them are related to English / German / French / Latin words? Which of their meanings can you guess from the context? Check with a dictionary.*

c) *Complete these exercises:*

1. Summarise the difficulties that hip-hop and rap artists from Scotland have to deal with.
2. Explain what Hang is, what it aims to do and which opportunities it offers.
3. Explain what makes the Scottish rap scene special and compare Scottish to English rap.

SPEAKING **d)** *Give a two-minute presentation on one of the artists from the text or any other Scottish musician.*

SKILLS 12 Working with words → SB 26/2; S2

a) *Say which dictionary you need in these situations.*

1. You are writing an essay and are looking for alternatives for the word "also". – ______________
2. You can't think of the English word for the German word "Brötchen". – ______________
3. You want to know how the word "literally" is used in context. – ______________
4. You don't understand the word "fauxpology" from a rap song. – ______________

b) *In your monolingual dictionary, check if these statements are true or false. Tick ✔ the correct answer and correct the wrong statements.*

	true	false
1. The last entry under 'X' is Xylophone. Correction: ______________		
2. 'Pike' is a noun and a verb. Correction: ______________		
3. Fit is not a noun. Correction: ______________		

c) *Match these phrasal verbs with their synonyms. Check with a dictionary which register they are.*

______ register	______ register
1. to hang out	a) to avoid
2. to get out of	b) to leave
3. to freak out	c) to spend time together
4. to take off	d) to tolerate
5. to put up with	e) to go crazy

d) *Compare the synonyms for the words **attractive** and **tired** and say in which context they are used. Then, in your exercise book, write example sentences for the synonyms in their context. Check with a dictionary for help.*

handsome | pretty | affordable

sleepy | bored | frustrated

SKILLS 13 Understanding the meaning → SB 26/2; S1

Read the text and have a closer look at the words and phrases in bold. Say what they mean, how you figured out their meaning (e.g. context, similar to another language, dictionary) and if they were difficult to figure out.

Sean Connery, **renowned** for his role as James Bond, dies age 90. The film icon **starred** in seven of the **spy** films. His audience especially **appreciated** his **confidence** and **sharp humour** as the **infamous agent**. Connery's other films included *Indiana Jones* and *Highlander.* Connery won an **Academy Award** for his role in *The Untouchables*. **Director** George Lucas, who created the *Indiana Jones* **franchise**, said that Connery had **left a mark** in **cinematic** history. Furthermore, Connery was a **patriotic** Scot and an **ardent advocate** of Scotland's independence.

VIEWING **14** ## Going downhill → SB 28/1; S19

V2

a) *Watch this clip about mountain biking in Scotland and tick ✔ the photos which show official trails at the Glentress Mountain Bike Trail Centre.*

b) *Watch the video again and name the disadvantages and advantages of unsanctioned[1] trails.*

disadvantages	advantages
– *liability[2] for when sb gets hurt*	

WRITING

c) *Write a comment (about 120 words) for a sports magazine in which you suggest solutions to the problem of unsanctioned mountain biking trails.*

SPEAKING **15** ## The Scottish oil and gas industry → SB 28/3; S18

a) *Look at the diagram and talk about it with your partner. Say what the diagram shows and mention important figures and developments.*

b) *Talk about reasons for these developments and possible consequences for the Scottish economy. Then research online and compare the results to your ideas.*

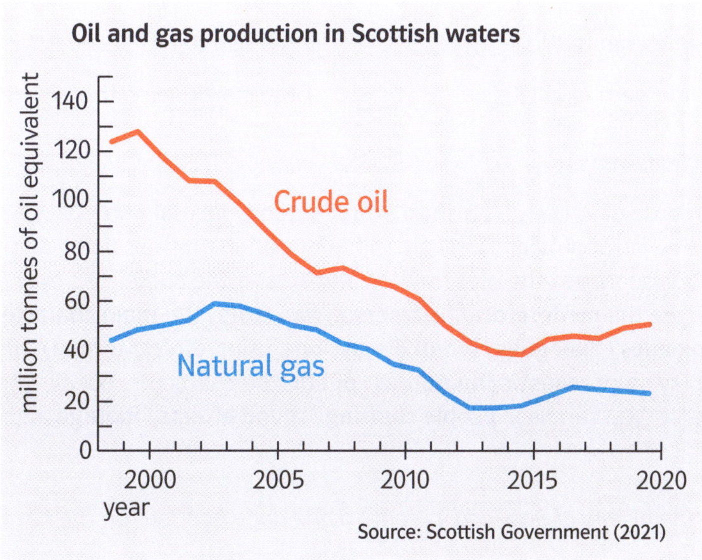

Useful phrases

The diagram shows how much … in … | … was highest / lowest in … | … has increased / decreased … | considerably / significantly / slightly | If you compare … | There is a general / downward trend … | A (possible) reason for this is / could be … | If this trend continues, this might result in … | Also this would (possibly) mean that …

1 unsanctioned [ˌʌnˈsæŋkʃnd] nicht zugelassen ○ **2** liability [ˌlaɪəˈbɪləti] Haftung

LISTENING **16** **The cattle of Pabbay** → SB 29/1; S13

A 5–6

a) *Listen to the Scottish story and complete the summary.*

Hamish and Bonnie moved to their own ___________ on a small _____________.

Surprisingly, they found a pregnant[1] ___________ in the barn. Soon they had a whole herd of ___________ with calves[2]. Many years later, Hamish wanted to ___________ Kelsie because she was getting old, but Kelsie and the herd ________________________________.

b) *Listen to part 1 and answer these questions. Take notes.*

1. What was the life of a Scottish crofter[3] like?

____

____

____

2. Why have landowners started to send away the crofters from their land?

____

3. How did life improve for Bonnie and Hamish after getting their own farm?

____

____

____

c) *Listen to part 2 and put the plot in the correct order. There is one extra sentence.*

- ☐ Hamish can't find Kelsie in the barn.
- ☐ Davina explains that magical cows have excellent hearing.
- ☐ Bonnie and Hamish run to the sea.
- ☐ Hamish enters the barn to kill Kelsie.
- ☐ Bonnie couldn't sleep all night.
- ☐ The moral is not to hurt anyone who has helped you.
- ☐ Hamish thinks Kelsie is too old.
- ☐ Davina explains that Kelsie is a magical cow.

d) *Underline the correct answer(s).*

The radio play "The cattle of Pabbay" is a **short story / legend / factual text** about a magical Scottish animal. The narrator provides background information on the setting and **author / text type / characters**, but also moves the plot forward and acts as the audience's **eyes / hands / mind**. Hamish and Bonnie are the **moderators / first-person narrators / the main characters** and talk with each other in **monologues / dialogues / group discussions**, using **direct / formal / informal** language. To make the radio play more **realistic / humorous / poetic**, the characters speak with an accent. As is typical for this genre, you can hear **people chatting / sound effects / footage** and music in the background.

WRITING

e) *For a project about the history of Scotland, prepare a one-page handout on the history of Scottish crofts.*

1 pregnant ['pregnənt] schwanger ○ **2** calf, calves *(pl)* [kɑːf; kɑːvz] Kalb, Kälber ○ **3** crofter [krɒftə] Kleinpächter/-in

VIEWING

17 The forgotten island of Belnahua → SB 29/1; S19

V3

a) *Watch the film about a Scottish island's industrial past and answer these questions. Take notes.*

1. Why is it so unusual that Belnahua used to be an industrial area?

____

____

____

2. How is Belnahua different to other industrial history sites, according to the presenter?

____

____

b) *Watch the video again and complete the text.*

While ______________ lives on Belnahua today and the island is overgrown by __________, its industrial past is still visible thanks to rusting ______________ and broken ______________. There used to be large ______________ that were over ______________ deep, now they're ______________. Not only did the workers have to do hard manual labour[1], but it was also often ______________. Because quarrying[2] a good piece of slate is difficult, rejected[3] pieces still lay ______________. In the late 1800s ______________ lived on Belnahua, among them Fiona Cruikshank's great aunt, who worked as ______________.

c) *Tick ✔ the correct answer(s).*

1. How were the conditions on the island?
   - a) ☐ desperate
   - b) ☐ noisy
   - c) ☐ grim[4]
   - d) ☐ lonely

2. Which problems did the islanders face?
   - a) ☐ slate dust
   - b) ☐ thieves
   - c) ☐ lack of freshwater
   - d) ☐ the tide

3. Where and what for was the slate from Belnahua used?
   - a) ☐ on Scottish castles
   - b) ☐ as decoration
   - c) ☐ in Nova Scotia
   - d) ☐ as roof material

1 manual labour ['mænjuəl ˌleɪbə] körperliche Arbeit ○ **2** to quarry ['kwɒri] (Stein) abbauen ○ **3** rejected [rɪ'dʒektɪd] ausgemustert ○
4 grim [grɪm] trostlos

LANGUAGE **18**

Mixed bag: Hogmanay → SB 29/1

Complete this newspaper article about Hogmanay with the missing words or phrases.

Scotland is a great place __________ on December __________! Hogmanay is __________ Scots word for the last day of the year and the traditional celebrations __________ go with it. These __________ visiting your family, giving gifts, and ______________ a meal together. If asked to name the __________ (good) festival of __________ year, many Scots ______________ it was Hogmanay. The __________ famous custom is 'first footing', __________ happens just after midnight. A friend or guest is asked __________ a piece of coal into your home for good luck. Shortbread, whisky or a 'black bun' (a type of fruit cake) may __________ be used ______________ coal. Another custom is singing 'Auld Lang Syne'. The title means 'since old times', ____________________ (refer) long friendship. Everybody links arms while ______________ the song together.

LANGUAGE **19**

Find the mistakes: More festivals in Scotland → SB 29/1

Read an article from a tourism website about Scottish celebrations. Decide if the underlined phrases are correct or not. Correct the mistakes.

After Hogmanay, the (1) famousest festival in the Scottish calendar is Burns Night on 25th January. This is the birthday of (2) Scotland poet Robert Burns (1759–1796), who (3) has also written the poem the song 'Auld Lang Syne' (4) is based of. The day (5) was celebrate with a 'Burns Supper', (6) which are haggis (a sheep's stomach (7) filling with meat and vegetables) served with turnips and (8) potatos.
Highland Games events (9) were held all around Scotland in the summer months. (10) The biggest takes place at the Cowal Highland Gathering, which (11) not only has hammer throw and caber toss, (12) as well as a pipe band competition and Highland dancing championships. For those who (13) will rather see something (14) moderner, Scotland's most important arts festival is (15) the Edinburgh Festival, (16) hold in August each year. (17) In fact, 'Edinburgh Festival' refers to a variety of different festivals. (18) Between them is the Fringe festival with (19) it's open stage that (20) had been the starting point for many now famous performers.

MEDIATION **20** **Bavarians – the Scots of Germany?** → SB 29/1; S16

For a project about Scotland in class you need to highlight similarities and differences between Scotland and Bavaria. Use this travel report to make a mind map for your project taking notes on different categories: culture, landscape, typical food, politics, economy.

Mit Dirndl in die Highlands

Studi-Blog: Emilia Porz; Studiengang: BWL
Beitrag vom 15.05.2021

Beim Kofferpacken gilt allgemein die Regel: Weniger ist mehr. Nicht jedoch bei meinem Praktikumsaufenthalt in Schottland. So sollte diesmal auch mein Dirndl, das ich sonst nur auf Volksfesten trage, mit auf Reisen gehen. Denn bei Feierlichkeiten trägt Schotte/Schottin und Bayer/-in auch gerne mal Tracht und die WG, in der ich zur Untermiete wohnen sollte, hatte bereits angekündigt, dass wir gemeinsam in unseren traditionellen Outfits zur „Royal Highland Show" in Edinburgh gehen würden.

Während meines Aufenthalts konnte ich schnell noch mehr Gemeinsamkeiten, aber auch Unterschiede feststellen. Die schottische sowie die bayerische Fahne sind weiß und blau. Wenn ich an weiß-blau in Bayern denke, dann kommt mir sofort ein Alpenpanorama mit strahlendem blauem Himmel und weißen Schäfchenwolken in den Sinn. In Schottland müsste man dieser Logik folgend die Flagge jedoch eher grau einfärben. Mit atemberaubenden Berglandschaften können aber beide punkten, ebenso mit traumhaften Burgen und weidenden Kühen. Ich muss dazu sagen, dass die schottischen Highlands viel mystischer und unergründlicher wirken. Das Mystische spiegelt sich auch in den Fabelwesen wider, die in Schottland (angeblich) leben – von Kelpies bis zum Loch Ness Monster. Im Vergleich dazu erscheint der bayerische Wolpertinger geradezu niedlich.

Sehr gemütlich fand ich auch die schottischen Winterfeste, zu denen „Burns Night" und „Hogmanay" gehören. Da kann man immer „Auld Lang Syne" anstimmen und sich bei anderen einhaken. Bei der „Burns Night" stand „Haggis" auf dem Speiseplan. Viele trauen sich nicht an das Nationalgericht aus Schafsinnereien. Klingt erstmal etwas eklig, aber Innereien habe ich bereits bei meinen Großeltern gegessen, deshalb hatte ich kein Problem damit. Geschmacklich hat es mich an Blutwurst erinnert, nochmal bestellen würde ich es allerdings eher nicht. Ganz anders sieht das beim schottischen Nationalgetränk Whisky aus. Der rauchige Whisky passt sehr gut zu Schottland. Im Gegenzug hatte ich meiner WG fränkisches Bier mitgebracht. Das fanden sie super!

Ich musste feststellen, dass es viele Klischees über Schotten/Schottinnen gibt und sie in einen Topf mit dem Rest von Großbritannien geworfen werden. Viele meiner Mitstudierenden, denen ich von meinem Praktikum erzählt habe, haben im Gespräch oft „England" statt „Schottland" gesagt. Ich habe sie dann immer sofort gerügt. Außerdem spielt nicht jeder hier Dudelsack und trägt jeden Tag Karo – mein Dirndl wird ja auch fast nur fürs Oktoberfest ausgepackt. Bayern und Schottland haben jeweils ihre eigene Kultur und sind nicht gleichzusetzen mit Deutschland bzw. Großbritannien. Das gilt auch für unsere Dialekte: wir werden nur schwer verstanden und dafür manchmal skeptisch angeschaut. Für uns spiegelt unser Dialekt unseren Stolz und die Liebe zur Heimat wider.

Dass Schottland und Bayern früher beide unabhängig waren und erst später Teil eines Nationalstaates wurden, erklärt wiederkehrende Debatten zur Unabhängigkeit. Obwohl Schottland weniger als die Hälfte der Bevölkerung Bayerns hat und auch wirtschaftlich lange nicht so gut dasteht, hat in Schottland 2014 ein Unabhängigkeitsreferendum stattgefunden. Fast 45 % haben dafür gestimmt. Seit dem Austritt Großbritanniens aus der EU hat das schottische Unabhängigkeitsbestreben noch einmal mehr Fahrt aufgenommen. Auch wenn Bayern immer wieder seine besondere Rolle in Deutschland betont, so ist die Sache hier ein bisschen komplizierter. Es gibt da nämlich gleich zwei Unabhängigkeitsbewegungen – eine bayerische und eine fränkische.

Ich bin immer noch begeistert davon, wie viel Bayern und Schottland verbindet, während sie zugleich politisch und wirtschaftlich unterschiedlich dastehen.

Einen Aufenthalt in Schottland kann ich deshalb jedem nur wärmstens empfehlen!

SPEAKING **21**
Life in Scotland
→ SB 29/1; S14, S17–18

a) ***Warm-up:*** *Together with a partner, talk about the questions.*

1. What comes to your mind when you think about Scotland? Name at least three aspects.
2. Would you like to live in Scotland? Say why you would (not) move.

b) ***Monologue:*** *Describe one of the photos of Scotland to your partner. Comment on the way of life there. Think of: lifestyle, culture, job opportunities, transport, cost of living, housing.*

Partner A Cottage in the Scottish Highlands

Partner B Glasgow city centre

c) ***Dialogue:*** *Together with your partner you want to do a two-week language course in Scotland. You can choose between four schools which are in Aberdeen, Glasgow, the Highlands and on the Shetland Islands. Discuss and then decide together on the location and when you want to go. Include the statistics in your discussion.*

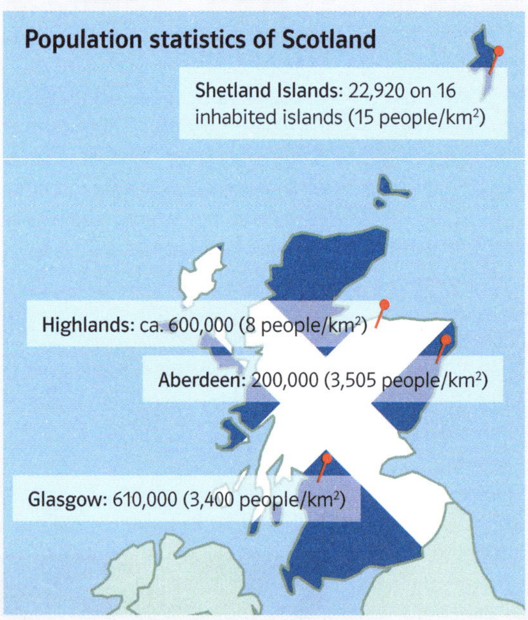

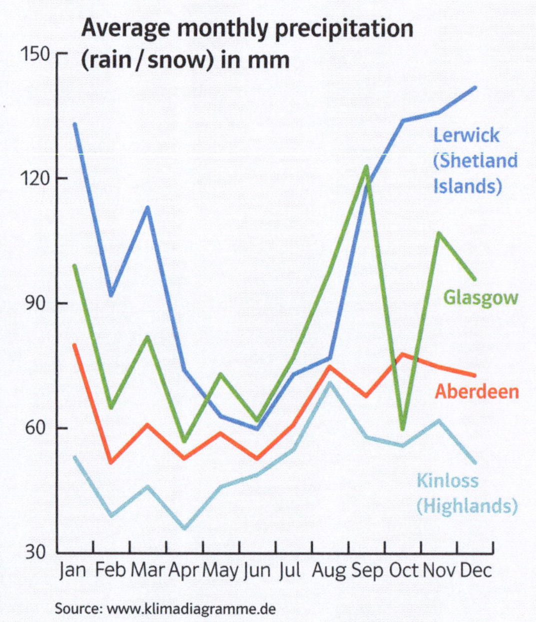

Source: www.klimadiagramme.de

Useful phrases

Opinion In my opinion … | I believe / feel / suppose … | My impression is that … | Personally, … | I would rather … | I'd prefer … | What do you think of …?

(Dis-)Agreeing I see your point. | That's a good point. | Actually, I think that … | I still have my doubts about … | I (dis-)agree because … | I completely (dis-)agree.

Statistics The statistics show … | Comparing … and …, it is clear that … | The figures / numbers show that … | It can be seen that … | a strong / slight increase / decrease | This means that …

Self-assessment

On this page you can assess your performance. Look at the exercises in this workbook unit again and colour the traffic lights in the grid. Which skill(s) would you like to improve? The last column will tell you where to find help in your book.

Skill	Exercise(s)	Check	Help
LISTENING / VIEWING			
I know how to ...			
– understand the gist and the detail in listening texts and video clips (e.g. comedy show, radio play, documentary).	6, 8 a)–d), 14 a)–b), 16 a)–d), 17	○ ○ ○	S6, S13, S19
READING			
I know how to ...			
– understand and analyse newspaper articles.	5 c)–f), 11 a)–c)	○ ○ ○	S5–6, S11
– understand and analyse extracts from a novel.	10 a), c)–g)	○ ○ ○	S5–6, S11
SPEAKING			
I know how to ...			
– have a discussion with a partner.	2 b), 3 b), 21 a)	○ ○ ○	S14
– describe, analyse and discuss statistics and diagrams.	4, 15, 21 c)	○ ○ ○	S18
– give a two-minute presentation.	11 d)	○ ○ ○	S15
– describe a picture.	21 b)	○ ○ ○	S17
WRITING			
I know how to ...			
– describe and analyse a cartoon.	2 a)	○ ○ ○	S17
– write an informative text.	5 g)	○ ○ ○	S7–9
– write a convincing letter.	8 e)	○ ○ ○	S7–9
– write a comment.	10 h), 14 c)	○ ○ ○	S7–12
– write a scene.	10 h)	○ ○ ○	S7–8
– write a handout.	16 e)	○ ○ ○	S15
MEDIATION			
I know how to ...			
– transfer relevant information into the target language in a way that is appropriate to the target audience and the situation.	3 a), 20	○ ○ ○	S5–6, S16
MEDIA COMPETENCE			
I know how to ...			
– use different types of dictionaries.	12	○ ○ ○	S2
VOCABULARY / GRAMMAR			
I know how to ...			
– use relevant vocabulary and appropriate grammar to talk and write about Scotland.	1, 7, 9, 18, 19	○ ○ ○	S1–2
– how to deal with unknown words.	5 b), 10 b), 13	○ ○ ○	S1–2

Focus 2 Scottish identity

READING **1** **Scottish independence** → SB 33/6; S7–10

a) *Read the texts and do the exercises below. Use a dictionary for help.*

A

Independence three times more expensive than Brexit

A study by the London School of Economics has concluded that the cost to the Scottish economy of independence would be two to three times larger than the cost of Brexit. A major reason is that Scotland's exports are 60 % to the rest of the UK, 19 % to the EU, 21 % to rest of the world. Independence would very probably make travel and trade between Scotland and England more difficult. However, most imports and exports would still have to come through England, resulting in higher costs for Scottish businesses.

B

@ZaMi2: Don't forget that most of the UK's oil reserves are off the coast of Scotland. That's worth millions for an independent Scotland! **564 likes**

C

"It would not be possible for [an independent Scotland] to avoid having to commit to the adoption of the euro; and if politicians were too vocal about their non-commitment to taking such a step, there is a danger that the EU might in the end not agree to Scottish membership." Tobias Locke, professor of law, the National University of Ireland Maynooth

D

2014 Independence referendum result and responses to a 2021 survey question 'Would you vote for Independence for Scotland?'

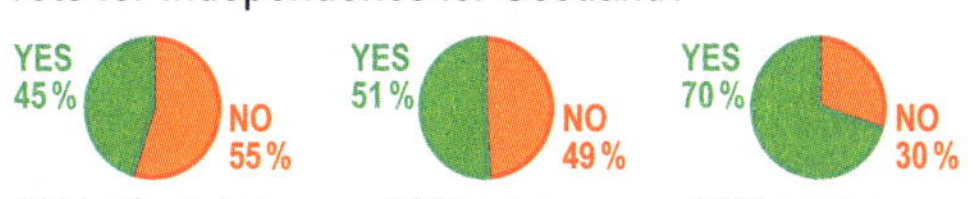

2014 referendum | 2021 survey, all voters | 2021 survey, voters aged 16–34

E

Hollie McIntyre says:
I understand your argument that the union with England has existed since 1707 and we share a language and our histories. But I strongly believe that with the independence from the UK, we will see a renaissance of our unique Scottish culture.
Reply

F

Results of the 2016 Brexit referendum

All of UK: Leave 52 % Remain 48 %
Scotland: Leave 38 % Remain 62 %

G

3 in 5 Scots want indyref2[1]

1 indyref = second referendum on Scottish independence

H

@hallie_duffy: We've had our own parliament since 1999, but our future is still decided in London. We need to decide on policies ourselves because we know best. **2365 likes**

I

Populations 2021 (in millions)

Scotland: 5.5 m
Ireland: 4.9 m
Denmark: 5.7 m
UK: 68.4 m

J

K

Rejoining the EU "might, at the fastest, take four to five years".

Dr Kirsty Hughes, Director of the Scottish Centre on European relations

b) *In your exercise book make mind maps on the topics of **politics** and **economy**. Use words and phrases from the texts and add your own.*

c) *Use two different colours to mark if the information given in texts A–K is a reason **for** or **against** Scotland becoming independent and rejoining the EU.*

WRITING **d)** *In your exercise book write an argumentative essay (about 220 words) on the question if Scotland should become independent and rejoin the EU. Exchange texts with a partner and peer-edit each other's work.*

VOCABULARY

1 What are you playing? → SB 34/2

Gary (G), a Scottish exchange student, is staying with Mike (M), a German student. Complete their conversation with the correct form of these words and phrases.

arrangement | bagpipes | to be into | to be played | beat | energetic | fiddle | Gaelic | to hear | to incorporate | influential | instrument | lyrics | pop | to put on | traditional | tradition | tune

M: What music are you listening to? It sounds very ________________.

G: Oh, I ________________ some ________________ Scottish folk music.

M: That's lovely! I didn't know you ________________ folk music.

G: I am! It has a long ________________ in Scotland. Often, folk music ________________ at social events, like at weddings or in pubs. Scottish folk songs come from melodies found in the ________________ tradition.

M: When I think of Scottish folk music, I only think of loud and shrill ________________.

G: Yes, they are almost symbolic for Scottish identity. But, there are other ________________ too, like the ____________ and wooden flute. I ____________ your parents listening to German folk music – it had a really strong ________________. I was surprised.

M: That was probably what we call *Schlager*. It ________________ some elements of traditional folk music, but with modern ________________ that use synthesisers.

G: Now I'm confused. How can you tell the difference between *Schlager* and folk music?

M: *Schlager* music is basically ________ music with a catchy ____________. The ____________ are usually quite simple and easy to remember. Folk music – or *Volksmusik* – is often about more serious topics. Traditional *Volksmusik* has been very ________________ in the way that German music has developed, but I think *Schlager* music is more popular.

WRITING

2 Folk and folk-inspired music in movies and shows → SB 35/4; S19

Choose a scene with folk or folk-inspired music from a movie or show. In your exercise book, write an analysis (about 200 words) on the effect the music has. Use these ideas or your own:

Emma (2020) | Sanditon (2019) | King Arthur: Legend of the Sword (2017) | O Brother, Where Art Thou? (2000)

Focus 3 Slavery and the Civil War

READING

1 Slave revolts → SB 38/3; S5

a) *Read the text and do the exercises in your exercise book.*

It is a mistaken belief that enslaved people did not resist[1] slavery. In fact, not only did enslaved people participate in passive resistance by arriving late to work or working slower than necessary, but they also practiced active resistance. This included damaging tools, running away, physically attacking their enslavers and participating in revolts.

One of the most well-known revolts – the Stono Rebellion – took place in South Carolina in 1739. Up to 100 enslaved African people participated and killed at least 20 white people. It is believed that the rebels tried to reach Florida, where the Spanish were promising runaways freedom and land. Militia killed at least 54 of the rebels and with that ended the revolt. The potential of revolts was a constant cause of worry for white enslavers and one result of the Stono Rebellion was an act which restricted the life of enslaved people even further. It prohibited them to get together in groups, grow their own food, earn money, learn how to write and to move freely. Another consequence had to do with the leaders of the Stono Rebellion being native Africans. Enslavers believed it would be better to only have enslaved people born in North America, arguing that if they had never known freedom, they would be less rebellious. As a result, slave imports were stopped in South Carolina. Using similar arguments, enslavers legally releasing enslaved people from slavery, known as manumission, became more difficult too. It was feared that free Black people would make enslaved people more rebellious.

However, none of this stopped slave uprisings. The Haitian Revolution (1791–1803), which is considered by some as the only successful slave revolt in history and which ended with the founding of an independent state by formerly enslaved people, inspired the largest slave revolt in the US – the German Coast Uprising of 1811. More than 500 enslaved people revolted in Louisiana, hoping to establish their own Black state. The revolt lasted two days in which the rebels burned down several plantations and killed two white people. The uprising was brutally defeated by U.S. troops and militia.

In 1831, the Nat Turner rebellion became the bloodiest uprising in US history for both Black and white people. On August 21st Nat Turner and six others killed Nat's enslaver and got hold of weapons. Over the course of two days, they managed to gather 75 other enslaved and free Black people and kill around 55 white people. They were eventually defeated by white authorities. The uprising caused even more mistrust between the two groups and in the aftermath, not only most of the rebels were killed, but it is estimated that also 200 Black people, who were not involved in the rebellion, were killed in the following days. Fuelled by the fear of further uprisings, more laws restricting the freedom of Black people were passed and pro-slavery and anti-abolitionist beliefs were strengthened.

Despite the chances being against them, enslaved people were willing to risk their lives because they had nothing to lose and only their freedom to win. Objectively, the enslaved people didn't stand a chance. Nevertheless, numerous rebellions that challenged slavery and its cruelty took place.

b) *Complete these exercises:*

1. Create a timeline of the slave revolts mentioned. Take notes on what happened.
2. Give examples on how white enslavers tried to defend the institution of slavery.
3. Explain why "objectively, the enslaved people didn't stand a chance".

SPEAKING

c) *Research more about the ways in which enslaved people showed resistance and give a three-minute presentation.*

1 to resist [rɪˈzɪst] sich widersetzen

LISTENING

2 Harriet Tubman – runaway, conductor[1] and spy → SB 38/5; S13

A7–8

a) *Listen to this online seminar about Harriet Tubman. In your exercise book, take notes on these important dates about Tubman.*

around 1820 | 1849 | 1850–1860 | 1862 | June 1963 | 1913

b) *Listen to part 1 and answer these questions. Take notes.*

1. What were the two things that helped Tubman on her escape? ____________________

____

2. What was the Underground Railroad, when did it run and what was its goal? ____________

____

c) *Are these statements true or false? Tick ✔ the correct answer.*

	true	false
1. The people who ran the Underground Railroad used secret codes, for example "baggage[2]" for escaping enslaved people.		
2. Tubman scheduled her trips according to the weather report in the Monday newspaper.		
3. The Fugitive Slave Act did not only make escaping more dangerous for enslaved people, but also for anyone who helped them.		

d) *Listen to part 2 and complete the text about Tubman's missions as a spy.*

Tubman, who was ______________ of a group of ____________ scouts[3], was very valuable to the Union Army. The antislavery activist was able to enter ____________________ by dressing up as a ______________ or ____________________. Because the ____________________________ trusted Tubman and her team, they ____________________________________

____.

Harriet Tubman
(colorized photo, 1895)

READING

3 A closer look at the Civil War → SB 38/5; S3, S21

a) *In groups, complete these steps to create a "collection of materials" for your classmates:*

1. Choose from one of these topics: one of the milestones of the Civil War, a person involved in the Civil War, the Reconstruction era after the Civil War.
2. Research your topic and create a collection of relevant materials (articles, videos, podcasts etc.).
3. Create a quiz on the materials in your collection.

Tip

Your collection should be about quality and not quantity.

b) *Choose two collections from the other groups. Go through the materials and complete the quizzes.*

1 conductor [kən'dʌktə] Zugführer/-in ○ 2 baggage ['bægɪdʒ] Gepäck ○ 3 scout [skaʊt] Kundschafter/-in

Unit 2 Black in America

VOCABULARY

1 Organising vocabulary → SB 40/2

a) *Find nouns or adjectives to make collocations to talk about the people of a country.*

1. ______________ + size, density, group
2. ______________ / ______________ + group, language, population
3. ______________ + society, population, background
4. ______________ + discrimination, segregation, equality
5. ______________ + background, minority, majority
6. ______________ + heritage, identity, diversity

b) *Use these words to write a wiki text (about 100 words) about the US population.*

WRITING

2 Census investigation → SB 40/2; S4, S17

a) *In your exercise book, describe and analyse the cartoon (about 120 words).*

b) *With a partner discuss if the census should ask for a person's race and which issues are connected to this question.*

c) *If you had to design the form for a census in the US, which other questions would you include and why?*

READING

3 A rescue mission gone wrong → SB 42/1; S5–6, S10–12

a) *Justyce (Jus) is a Black seventeen-year-old teenager from Atlanta. One night when he's looking for his ex-girlfriend Melo (Mel), things don't go as planned. Read the novel excerpt and do the exercises.*

From where he's standing across the street, Justyce can see her: Melo Taylor, ex-girlfriend, collapsed beside her Benz on the concrete of the FarmFresh parking lot. She's missing a shoe, and the contents of her purse are spread out around her like the guts of a pulled party popper[1]. He knows she's drunk, but this is too much, even for her. As he approaches, she opens her eyes, and he waves and pulls his earbuds out just in time to hear her say, "What the hell are you doing here?"

Justyce asks himself the same question as he watches her try – and fail – to shift to her knees. She falls over sideways and hits her face against the car door.

He drops down and reaches for her cheek. "Damn, Melo, are you okay?"

She pushes his hand away. "What do you care?"

Stung, Justyce takes a deep breath. He cares a lot. Obviously. If he didn't, he wouldn't've walked a mile at three in the morning. All to keep his drunken disaster of an ex from driving. He should walk away right now. But he doesn't.

"Jessa called me," he tells her.

"That skank[1]–"

Justyce shakes his head. "I just came to make

1 party popper ['pɑ:ti ˌpɒpə] Partyknaller

sure you get home okay."

That's when it hits Justyce that while he might succeed in getting Melo home, he has no idea how he'll get back. He looks Melo over.

She's now sitting with her head leaned back against the car door, half-asleep, mouth open. She starts to slide sideways, and Justyce catches her by the shoulders to keep her from falling. She startles, looking at him wide-eyed, and Jus can see everything about her that initially caught his attention. That's part of his problem: he gets too tripped up[2] by how beautiful she is.

She starts shifting her stuff around on the ground. "Ugh, where are my keeeeeeeys?"

Justyce sees them in front of the back tire and picks them up. "You're not driving, Melo."

"Give 'em." She reaches for the keys but falls into his arms instead. Justyce leans her against the car again and gathers the rest of her stuff to put it back in her bag. He, unlocks the car, throws the bag on the floor of the backseat, and tries to get Melo up off the ground. Then everything goes really wrong, really fast.

First, she throws up all over the hoodie Jus is wearing. When he tries to pick Melo up again, she slaps him. Hard. "Leave me alone, Justyce," she says.

"I can't do that, Mel. There's no way you'll make it home if you try to drive yourself."

He tries to pick her up by the armpits and she spits in his face. He considers walking away again. He could call her parents, put her keys in his pocket, and leave. Oak Ridge is probably *the* safest neighborhood in Atlanta. She'd be fine for the twenty-five minutes it would take Mr. Taylor to get here. But he can't. Leaving her here all vulnerable[3] doesn't seem like the right thing to do. So he picks her up and throws her over his shoulder.

Melo reacts in her usual delicate fashion[4]: she screams and beats him on the back with her fists.

Justyce struggles to get the back door open and is lowering her into the car when he hears the WHOOOOP of a short siren and sees the blue lights. In the few seconds it takes the police car to screech[5] to a stop behind him, Justyce settles Melo into the backseat. Now she's gone catatonic[6].

Justyce can hear the approaching footsteps, but he stays focused on getting Melo strapped

in[7]. He wants it to be *clear* to the cop that she wasn't gonna drive so she won't be in even worse trouble.

Before he can get his head out of the car, he feels a pull on his shirt and is yanked backward. His head hits the doorframe just before a hand clamps down on[8] the back of his neck. His upper body slams onto the trunk[9] with so much force[10], he bites the inside of his cheek, and his mouth fills with blood.

Jus swallows, head spinning. The sting of cold metal around his wrists pulls him back to reality. Handcuffs[11].

The cop shoves him to the ground beside the police car as he asks if Justyce understands his rights. Justyce doesn't remember hearing any rights, but his ears *had* been ringing from the two hits to the head, so maybe he missed them. He swallows more blood.

"Officer, this is a big misundersta–" he starts to say, but he doesn't get to finish because the officer hits him in the face.

"Don't you say shit to me, you son of a bitch. I knew your punk ass was up to no good when I saw you walking down the road with that goddamn hood[12] on."

So the hood was a bad idea. Earbuds too. Probably would've noticed he was being followed without them. "But, Officer, I–"

"You keep your mouth *shut*." The cop squats[13] and gets right in Justyce's face. "I know your kind: punks like you wander the streets of nice neighborhoods searching for prey[14]. Just couldn't stay away from the pretty white girl who'd locked her keys in her car, could ya?"

Except that doesn't even make sense. If Mel had locked the keys in the car, Jus wouldn't have been able to get her inside it, would he? Justyce finds the officer's nameplate; CASTILLO,

1 skank *(sl)* ['skæŋk] Schimpfwort ○ **2** to get tripped up about *(infml)* [ˌget 'trɪpt ʌp ə'baʊt] durch etwas aus der Fassung gebracht werden ○ **3** vulnerable ['vʌlnrəbl] hilflos ○ **4** fashion ['fæʃn] Art und Weise ○ **5** to screech [skri:tʃ] quietschen ○ **6** catatonic [ˌkætə'tɒnɪk] leblos ○ **7** to strap sb in ['stræp ɪn] jdn. anschnallen ○ **8** to clamp down on sth [ˌklæmp 'daʊn ɒn] *hier:* (sich) festklemmen ○ **9** trunk [trʌŋk] Kofferraum ○ **10** force [fɔ:s] Kraft ○ **11** handcuffs *(pl)* [hændkʌfs] Handschellen ○ **12** hood [hʊd] Kapuze ○ **13** to squat [skwɒt] in die Hocke gehen ○ **14** prey [preɪ] Beute it reads, though the guy looks like a regular white dude. Mama told him what to do in this type of situation, though he must admit he never expected to actually need the advice: *Be respectful; keep the anger under control; make sure the police can see your hands* (though that's impossible right now). "Officer Castillo, I mean you no disresp–"

"I told your punk ass to shut the fuck up!" He wishes he could see Melo. Get her to tell this cop the truth. But the dude is blocking his view. "Now, if you know what's good for you, you won't move or speak. Resistance will only land you in deeper shit. Got it?"

Cigarette breath and spit hit Justyce's face as the cop speaks, but Justyce fixes his gaze[1] on the glowing green F of the FarmFresh sign.

"Look at me when I'm talking to you, boy." He grabs Justyce's chin. "I asked you a question."

Justyce swallows. Meets the cold blue of Officer Castillo's eyes. Clears his throat.

"Yes sir," he says. "I got it."

From: Nic Stone, *Dear Martin* (adapted)

b) *Find the words referring to body parts in the text. Then, in your exercise book, create a sketch of a human body on which you mark them. Use a dictionary for help.*

c) *Use the context to guess the meaning of these verbs and match them with the definitions.*

1. to startle (l. 37)
2. to slap (l. 54)
3. to yank (l. 84)
4. to slam (l. 87)
5. to shove (l. 93)

a) to hit sb with the flat part of the hand
b) to move suddenly as in surprise
c) to pull on sth hard and quickly
d) to push sb in a rough way
e) to push sb into a certain position with strength causing a loud noise

d) *Answer these questions. Write notes.*

1. Why is Justyce looking for his ex-girlfriend and what does this say about his character and his feelings for her? ______________________________
____
2. What are Melo's reactions to Justyce trying to help? ______________________________
____
____
3. Why does the police officer arrest Justyce? ______________________________
____
4. What is Justyce wearing and why is it important for what happened? ______________________________
____
____

e) *Name the main theme of the excerpt:*

____

Tip

A story often has more than one theme. Make a list of the themes that can be found in the excerpt. To find the main theme, identify the conflict of and / or meaning behind the story.

1 gaze [geɪz] Blick

f) *Justyce becomes a victim of police brutality. Give examples of police brutality from the text.*

Tip

Police brutality is the use of unnecessary force against a civilian that would be needed to protect someone or control a situation. It can be physical (e.g. beatings, murder) and nonphysical (e.g. harassment[1], verbal abuse[2]).

physical police brutality	nonphysical police brutality

g) *In your exercise book, compare and comment on Justyce's and Officer Castillo's behaviour.*

SPEAKING

h) *Choose **one** of the following tasks and give a five-minute presentation.*

1. Research and present a case of police brutality in the US.
2. Present and analyse the official book trailer of *Dear Martin.*

LANGUAGE

4 Find the mistakes: I Promise School → SB 46/4

Read this article about LeBron James and his foundation[3]. Decide if the underlined parts are correct or not. Correct the mistakes.

LeBron James, who is considered (1) being one of the best basketball players, (2) wanted to give back to (3) its community in Akron, Ohio. LeBron James acknowledges that if his talent (4) hadn't been recognized by a school in Akron and if he hadn't received extra support, he (5) will never make it. So, in 2004, the LeBron James Family Foundation (6) had been founded. One of the (7) foundations biggest projects is the "I Promise School". The students (8), who get accepted to (9) school are all "at-risk". Kids who at a very young age (10) has been identified already as in danger of (11) not complete high school. (12) Being part of the public school system, the "I Promise School" has a (13) $2 millions budget (14), which is about the same (15) than other schools. However, it (16) is given financial help by the foundation for additional teaching staff meant (17) reducing class sizes. Plus, the school (18) is offering extra resources for parents – classes to prepare them to get (19) there high school diplomas, for example.

1 harassment [hə'ræsmənt] Schikane ○ 2 abuse [ə'bju:s] Missbrauch ○ 3 foundation [faʊn'deɪʃn] Stiftung

LISTENING

5 The Nickel – from zydeco[1] music to football saints[2] → SB 47/5; S13

A 9–10

a) *Listen to this guided tour through Houston's Fifth Ward[3]. Bring the things the guide talks about in the correct order. There is one extra.*

A. ☐ active political groups
B. ☐ system and impact of redlining
C. ☐ founding of the ward
D. ☐ the ward's greatest decades
E. ☐ renewal and renovation
F. ☐ impact of a bridge

b) *Listen to part 1 and answer these questions in your exercise book. Take notes.*

1. When was the ward officially founded, who moved there and why?
2. What made the ward's school one of the best Black high schools and why isn't it one anymore?
3. Why did many Creoles leave the Mississippi River Valley and how did they influence the ward?

c) *Listen to part 2 and underline the correct answers. Sometimes more than one can be correct.*

1. The bridge divided the ward because
   it made the areas next to it less attractive. | it separated residential areas[4] from its business district. | the residents' opinions on the design of the bridge were very different.
2. The purpose of redlining was to
   make sure (white) people kept their homes. | only lend money to poor people. | create a ranking on how risky investments were in an area.
3. Redlining made it impossible for Black people to
   borrow money from the bank to buy a house. | move out of a red area. | get financial support from the government.

d) *Listen again and complete this text about the impact of redlining.*

Owning a house is important for ______________________________. A lack of ownership leads to a lack in ______________________________ and lack of ______________________________ ______________________________. In Houston ________% of white people are homeowners, compared to ________% of Black people.

e) *Choose **one** of the projects and take notes on how it impacts the ward positively:* **A:** Fifth Ward Community Redevelopment Corporation, **B:** DeLuxe Theater, **C:** Fifth Ward Saints football team.

____

____

____

SPEAKING

6 Growing up Black → SB 47/5; S3, S15

a) *Search online for memes and short videos on the topic "Growing up Black". Present one meme or video to the class and explain why the situation is typical of "Growing up Black": Which aspect of Black culture is being portrayed (e.g. identity, food, family)? What makes it funny?*

b) *Compare the memes/videos to your own experiences. Then discuss the pros and cons of making and sharing such visuals. (Think about individual experiences, stereotypes, gender roles etc.)*

1 zydeco ['zaɪdə‿koʊ] *schneller, rhythmischer Musikstil mit Akkordeon und Waschbrett* ○ **2** saint [seɪnt] Heilige/-r ○ **3** ward [wɔːd] Bezirk ○
4 residential area [ˌrezɪ'dentʃl ˌeəriə] Wohngebiet

LISTENING

7 Black History Month → SB 48/1; S13

A 11–12

a) *Listen to Jackson from the student council talk to the history teacher Mr. Lowe about Black History Month (BHM) during assembly. Tick ✔ the statement that sums up the assembly best.*

1. ☐ Mr. Lowe talks about Black people whom everyone should know and the future of BHM.
2. ☐ Mr. Lowe talks about the history of BHM, critically discusses BHM and makes suggestions on how to do things differently.
3. ☐ Mr. Lowe talks about the historical impact of BHM and why it is very different today compared to when it was first celebrated.

b) *Listen to part 1. Are these statements true or false? Tick ✔ the correct answer.*

	true	false
1. BHM goes back to an idea from 1926 by the historian Carter G. Woodson.	☐	☐
2. Woodson chose February to celebrate BHM because it's the birthday month of Lincoln and Douglass.	☐	☐
3. The first response to Woodson's idea was quite positive, especially in former slave states and cities.	☐	☐
4. BHM was officially recognised in 1969 by former president Gerald Ford.	☐	☐

c) *Listen to part 2 and complete these sentences.*

1. BHM has grown beyond schools, which means that ______________________

____

2. According to Jackson, BHM is used by businesses ______________________

____

3. A lot of people argue that Black history ______________________.

4. Some critics say that when February is over, ______________________

____

5. Mr. Lowe believes that Black history ______________________

____

d) *Answer these questions in your exercise book. Take notes.*

1. Why does Mr. Lowe criticise focussing on well-known figures from the civil rights movement only during BHM?
2. What does Mr. Lowe suggest doing better in general and for the student council specifically? (four things)
3. What does Mr. Lowe mean when he says "knowledge brings understanding"?

SPEAKING

e) *Get together in groups and do research on one of these important periods in Black history. Choose a digital tool (e.g. to create a website or video) or give a presentation to present your results.*

Middle Passage | Harlem Renaissance | Great Migration | Jim Crow Era

READING

8 Analysing a poem → SB 48/1; S5–7, S10–11

Read the poem and write an analysis (about 220 words) of it in your exercise book. Follow the steps.

The Bronze Legacy[1]

To a Brown Boy

'Tis a noble gift to be brown, all brown,
Like the strongest things that make up this earth,
Like the mountains grave[2] and grand[3],
Even like the very land,
Even like the trunks[4] of trees –
Even oaks[5], to be like these!
God builds His strength in bronze.

To be brown like thrush[6] and lark[7]!
Like the subtle wren[8] so dark!
Nay[9], the king of beasts wears brown;
Eagles are of this same hue.
I thank God, then, I am brown.
Brown has mighty[10] things to do.

Effie Lee Newsome, 1922

1. Say what the poem is about, how the title relates to the main theme and whom it is written for.
2. Identify the rhyme scheme and say what effect it has.
3. Analyse the language. Give evidence.
4. Research the historical context of the poem and say how this contributes to the message of the poem.

SPEAKING

9 Black representation in the film industry → SB 49/2; S18

a) *Black talent is underrepresented in film, especially off-screen. With your partner, compare the information given on the different genres and sum up the chart in one sentence.*

Genre	Share of all films	Examples	Average production budget	Share of category with 2+ Black off-screen talent*
Race specific (i.e., biography or documentary)	15 %	- Lincoln - Selma - Walk the line	22 million $	6 %
Race adjacent (i.e., comedy; race is often essential to topic or style)	18 %	- Barbershop 3 - Crazy Rich Asians - Knives out	23 million $	6 %
Race agnostic (i.e., all other genres; race is not important to topic or style)	67 %	- A Star is born - Red Notice - The Martian	64 million $	3 %

*The average film typically has six professionals in total across the key off-screen roles of producer, writer and director.

Source: McKinsey & Company, Variety Insight by Variety Business Intelligence

b) *Get together in groups and choose a movie produced in the US, identify which of the three genres it belongs to and find out more about the racial mix off-screen and its budget. Compare your findings to the chart and to the findings of the other groups.*

c) *In your group discuss why off-screen representation is just as important as on-screen representation.*

1 legacy ['legəsi] Vermächtnis **2** grave [greɪv] massiv **3** grand [grænd] prächtig **4** trunk [trʌŋk] Stamm **5** oak [əʊk] Eiche **6** thrush [θrʌʃ] Drossel **7** lark [lɑ:k] Lerche **8** wren ['ren] Zaunkönig **9** nay [neɪ] ja sogar **10** mighty [maɪti] mächtig

VIEWING **10** ## Black People Made That! → SB 50/3; S19

V4

a) *Watch the episode of* Say It Loud! *in which Azie and Evelyn talk about Black inventions and the US patent system*[1]*. Complete what Azie says about the historical conditions for Black inventors in the US.*

Even though Black enslaved people invented ______________________________,

______________ made it impossible for them to patent and ______________

of their inventions.

b) *Complete the grid about inventions by Black people during time of slavery.*

inventor	invention	what happened to the invention
Ned		
Henry Boyd		
Benjamin T. Montgomery		
Benjamin Bradley		

c) *Tick ✔ the correct statements about the information given on the US patent economy.*

1. ☐ Applications can take up to two years to become patent protected and can cost more than $15,000.
2. ☐ Because there is no data collected on who applies for patents, it is difficult to understand who is creating patents and to make sure that there are enough opportunities for diverse applicants.
3. ☐ The ethnicity of innovators born in the US is around 92% white compared to only 0.4% Black.
4. ☐ The patent economy is important not only because it contributes about one third to the US GDP[2], but also because it helps the US to keep its lead in innovation and creates millions of jobs.
5. ☐ IP-intensive industries make use of intellectual property[3] rights (e.g. patents, copyright, design).

d) *Watch the video again and, in your exercise book, analyse how it is made.*

1. Divide the video into parts and explain which purpose the different parts have.
2. Describe the style of the video and say which audience it was made for.

1 patent system [ˌpætnt ˈsɪstəm] Patentwesen **2** GDP (= gross domestic product) [ˌdʒiːdiːˈpiː] BIP (= Bruttoinlandsprodukt)
3 intellectual property [ˌɪntlˈektjuəl ˈprɒpəti] geistiges Eigentum

LANGUAGE

11 Mixed bag: Good Black News → SB 51/1

Complete this text about the website Good Black News.

The website *Good Black News* ______________________ in 2010 by an African-American woman who ________________ how difficult it was _____________ good news about Black people _______ major news sites. Lori Lakin Hutcherson ______________________ for news coverage[1] of a Black boys' school that sent 100 % of _______ graduates on to college, _______ she couldn't find any mention of the story – neither in _________ mainstream press _______ on Black sites. _______________ sitting back and accepting this, she decided ______________________ about it and ______________________ a platform dedicated to ______________________ positive news about African-Americans. She started with a social media page, _____________, after __________________ thousands of followers, eventually _______________ its own website. The site doesn't have _______ advertising at all and everyone volunteers their time. The site's goals _______ to educate and to highlight the positive and outstanding things _________ Black people do _________ day.

VOCABULARY

12 Organising vocabulary → SB 52/2

a) *In your exercise book, make a grid with these headings:*
talking about change | talking about racism | being a politician.
Then put these phrases in the correct group and add at least three of your own to each group.

to advocate reform | to become legal | to bring about change | cultural appropriation | to improve access | leadership role | movement | oppressive system | political standing | progress | to promise a positive outcome | public agenda | racial injustice | to reclaim one's identity | to represent a community | representation of minorities | violence | to win office

b) *Complete this speech by a local politician with words and phrases from a).*

It is about time that we bring an end to police _________________ and racial ______________. I am tired of being the victim of an______________________ that violates our rights as US citizens again and again. My ___________________________ has always been one of _________________ – improving our future instead of holding onto the past. And if I ________________ in the upcoming elections, I promise I _________________________ ____________________ that we all have been so desperately waiting for.

1 coverage ['kʌvərɪdʒ] Berichterstattung

MEDIATION 13 Racism in German football → SB 53/3; S16

The class of your British friend Yun does a project on racism in sports and she has to give a presentation on racism in football. Use the article to send her an e-mail (about 190 words) in which you tell her about racism in football in Germany and how some of the players affected dealt with it. Also explain to her why it might be a good idea to include a trigger warning before her presentation.

Diskriminierungen und Demütigungen

Alle waren von Rassismus betroffen: Der Dokumentarfilm "Schwarze Adler" erzählt von den Erfahrungen, die People of Color im deutschen Fußballnationalteam gemacht haben.

Der Triggerhinweis zu Beginn ist etwas ungelenk: "Der folgende Dokumentarfilm zeigt womöglich traumatisierende Inhalte wie rassistische Beleidigungen, Übergriffe und rassistisch motivierte Gewalt. Bitte stellen Sie sicher, dass Sie und Ihr Umfeld sich darauf einstellen, wenn Sie sich den Film ansehen." Aber dass es diesen Hinweis gibt, spricht für ein gestiegenes Bewusstsein im Umgang mit den Rassismen in der eigenen Geschichte. Denn wo in der deutschen Rezeption solche Kommunikationsformen zumeist abgetan wurden als vermeintlicher Ausdruck übertriebener Verzärtelung, signalisiert der Hinweis tatsächlich die Schwierigkeit, von Abwertung zu sprechen, ohne Abwertung damit zu wiederholen. Das ist die Herausforderung, die Torsten Körners Dokumentarfilm *Schwarze Adler* besteht, wenn er von People of Color im Trikot der deutschen Fußballnationalteams erzählt.

Das Bestechende an dem Film ist seine Perspektive. Der Blick geht hier vorbei an den Beckenbauers, Neids und Kahns, um auf eine Geschichte zu stoßen, die bislang Randnotiz oder Fußnote war. 14 Fußballstars geben Auskunft vor der Kamera, von Erwin Kostedde (Jahrgang 1946) bis Jean-Manuel Mbom (Jahrgang 2000), über Steffi Jones und Shary Reeves sowie Anthony Baffoe oder Guy Acolatse, der 1963 für den St. Pauli spielte. Alle eint, dass sie von Rassismus betroffen waren; verschieden sind die Formen des Umgangs damit, die Entscheidungen, zu denen individuelle Prägungen geführt haben.

So synthetisiert sich Geschichte. Erwin Kostedde bewundert das Selbstbewusstsein von Jimmy Hartwig, der im Nationaltrikot doch wiederum Kosteddes Schicksal teilt (keinen Platz zu finden) und sich deshalb über das gelungene Debüt von Gerald Asamoah Jahre später freut. Dessen einstiger Mitspieler Otto Addo will aufgrund rassistischer Diskriminierungen gar nicht für Deutschland spielen und begreift erst später, wie wichtig es war, dass Asamoah sich anders, gegen Ghana, entschieden hat – welche Vorbild- und Signalwirkung von ihm ausgegangen ist.

Immer wieder geht es um die Frage, wie das, was man schlucken muss, verdaut werden soll. Ob man wie Shary Reeves an das Ende der Kräfte gelangt, als der Trainer Gero Bisanz ihr in Aussicht stellt, nie für das Frauenteam zu spielen, weil sie doch gar nicht von hier sei. Oder wie Asamoah in die weiße Institution hineingeht, um die Arbeit zu leisten, die einerseits geleistet werden muss, andererseits aber doch eigentlich von dieser Institution selbst.

Zu dem differenzierten Bild von 70 Jahren deutschem Nachkriegsfußball, das *Schwarze Adler* zeichnet, gehört dazu, dass ein Happy End nicht leicht zu haben ist. Was etwa Asamoahs Geschichte zeigt, der Deutschland aus dem Otto-Katalog kannte, ehe er als Neunjähriger ins Land kam. Der schnell feststellte, dass nicht nur die Idioten das N-Wort benutzten, sondern alle. Und der auch nach der WM-Euphorie von 2006 in Stadien wieder auf Schmählaute traf.

Und krasser noch: Fünf Jahre nach Asamoahs emotionalem Abschied von den Schalker Fans, bei dem er dem vollen Stadion dankte, ihn immer als "einen von uns" begriffen zu haben, wird in jenem Stadion Herthas Jordan Torunarigha von den Rängen mit Demütigungen bedacht, die ihn verzweifelt eine Getränkekiste umschmeißen lassen. Schiedsrichter Harm Osmers (der trotz Hinweisen aus Herthas Team nichts mitbekommen haben will) entschied auf Platzverweis.

Hoch anzurechnen ist *Schwarze Adler*, dass er seine Geschichte im Resonanzraum des Essayistischen entwirft. Am schärfsten kann das weiße Deutschland sich deshalb in dem Archivmaterial erkennen, das von Bildern eines Spiels der deutschen Nationalmannschaft unter dem Trainer Sepp Herberger aus der NS-Zeit über Waschmittelwerbungen und abwertende Kabarettauftritte der Sechzigerjahre bis zu den Sportsendungen der Gegenwart reicht.

Matthias Dell, Zeit Online, 2021 (adaptiert)

SKILLS 14 Different (online) sources → SB 55/1

Complete this grid. Say for which purpose(s) these texts were created and how reliable they are. Say why you think they are (not) reliable.

source	purpose	reliability
1. popular science book on astronomy		
2. article about a workers' strike in a tabloid		
3. factual article about health by a fitness company		
4. sponsored product review on a blog		
5. social media post from a government institution		

SKILLS 15 Talking about false information → SB 55/2

a) *Write a glossary for these words in your exercise book.*

bot | clickbait | conspiracy theory | deepfake | fake news | satire | troll

b) *With a partner, discuss which of the terms you find most problematic.*

c) *Use a digital tool to do a survey in your class on how often you encounter the things from a). Discuss the results.*

SKILLS 16 Finding good (online) sources → SB 55/3; S3

a) *Choose one of these topics to do some research. Select four to five (online) sources that you could use to prepare a presentation on that topic.*

court case Brown vs. Board of Education | artwork Migration Series by Jacob Lawrence | athlete Jesse Owens | music show *Soul Train*

Tip

Reread through the tips for doing research on the poster or digital information sheet that you created.

b) *Get together in groups with the students who chose the same topic. Discuss your sources.*

READING **17** **Becoming Michelle Obama** → SB 57/1; S4–6, S10–11

a) *In her autobiography "Becoming", Michelle Obama tells the story of her life and how she became who she is – from growing up on Chicago's not-always-safe South Side until the day she left the White House, where she had been First Lady for eight years. Read this excerpt from her childhood and do the exercises. (Dandy is Michelle's grandfather and Craig her brother.)*

If my questions for Dandy were hard and unanswerable, I soon learned that many questions are just that way. In my own life, I was starting to encounter questions I couldn't easily answer. One came from a girl whose name I can't remember – one of the distant cousins who played with us in the backyard of one of my great-aunts' houses farther west of us. As the adults drank coffee and laughed in the kitchen, Craig and I would join whatever pack of kids came with those adults. Sometimes it was awkward, all of us managing a forced friendship, but generally it worked out. Craig almost always disappeared into a basketball game, I'd jump double Dutch or try to fall into whatever conversation was going on.

One summer day when I was about ten, I sat on a stoop, chatting with a group of girls my age. We were all in pigtails and shorts and basically just killing time. What were we discussing? It could have been anything – school, our older brothers, an anthill on the ground.

At one point, one of the girls gave me a sideways look and said, just a bit hotly, "How come you talk like a white girl?"

I could tell that she was trying to insult me, or at least challenge me, but that she was also curious to know why the two of us sounded different. We seemed to be related but of two different worlds.

"I don't," I said, looking scandalized that she'd even suggest it and embarrassed by the way the other girls were now staring at me.

But I knew what she was getting at. There was no denying it, even if I just had. I did speak differently than some of my relatives, and so did Craig. Our parents had drilled into us the importance of using correct diction, of saying "going" instead of "goin'" and "isn't" instead of "ain't." We were taught to finish off our words. They bought us a dictionary and a full Encyclopaedia Britannica set, which lived on a shelf in the stairwell to our apartment. Any time we had a question about a word, or a concept, or some piece of history, they directed us toward those books.

Dandy, too, was an influence, correcting our grammar or ordering us to enunciate our words when we went over for dinner. Dandy and my parents wanted us to have more opportunities than they had. They'd planned for it. They encouraged it. We were expected not just to be smart but to own our smartness – to inhabit it with pride – and this filtered down[1] to how we spoke. Yet it also could be a problem. Speaking a certain way – the "white" way, as some would have it – was seen as a betrayal, as being uppity, as somehow denying our culture.

Years later, after I'd met and married my husband – a man who is light-skinned to some and dark-skinned to others, who speaks like an Ivy League-educated Black Hawaiian raised by white middle-class Kansans – I'd see this confusion play out on the national stage among whites and Blacks alike. I'd see the need people have to define others by their ethnicity or the color of their skin. America would bring to Barack Obama the same questions my cousin was unconsciously[2] putting to me that day on the stoop: Are you what you appear to be? Do I trust you or not?

I passed the rest of that day trying to say less to my cousin, feeling put off[3] by her hostility, but also wanting her to see me as genuine[4] – not trying to show off some advantage. It was hard to know what to do. All the while, I could hear the sound of conversation going on between the adults in the kitchen nearby, my parents' laughter ringing easy and loud over the yard. I watched my brother in the flow of a sweaty game with a group of boys on the street corner. Everyone seemed to fit in, except for me. I look back on the discomfort of that moment now and recognize the more universal challenge of figuring out how who you are fits with where you come from and where you want to go. I also realize that I was a long way, still, from finding my voice.

From: Michelle Obama, *Becoming: Adapted for young readers* (adapted)

1 to filter down ['fɪltə daʊn] durchsickern ○ **2** unconsciously [ʌnˌkɒnʃəsli] unbewusst ○ **3** to feel put off [fiːl 'pʊt ˌɒf] sich abgeschreckt fühlen ○ **4** genuine ['dʒenjuɪn] aufrichtig

b) *Find the words in the text and write them under the correct pictures.*

1

2

3

4

5

c) *Find the words in the text for these definitions:*

1. way in which words are pronounced: ______________________
2. to pronounce words clearly: ______________________
3. behaving as if you are more important than others: ______________________
4. unfriendly or aggressive behaviour: ______________________

d) *Summarise the excerpt in two to three sentences.*

e) *Get together with a partner. Each partner answers* **one** *set of questions (***A** *or* **B***) in their exercise book. Peer-edit each other's texts.*

A 1. Explain why Michelle would think that when one of her cousins asks her why she talks "like a white girl" (l. 24) that she is trying to insult or at least challenge Michelle.
2. Describe how Michelle reacted to that question and explain why she reacted the way she did.

B 1. Explain why it is important for Michelle's parents and her grandfather that she and her brother learn correct diction.
2. Comment on how "talking like a white girl" (l. 24) is used as an equivalent for "talking in an educated way" in the excerpt.

f) *In your exercise book, analyse the connection between language and identity in the excerpt.*

Tip
Think about language as a part of an individual identity, but also as a shared feature. Identity can be perceived from the inside and outside.

READING **18**

Black Parents Give Their Kids 'The Talk.' What If White Parents Did, Too?

→ SB 57/1; S5–6

a) *Read the newspaper article and do the exercises on the following page.*

My mom and dad schooled me in life lessons that still echo through my mind. Among those lessons is "The Talk." Every Black child's parent knows it from when their parent sat them down for "The Talk." That's when they were told what to do – and what not to do – when the police show up.

Black parents know their child's life could depend on it. It could be the only thing that saves them in that flash of a moment. I was reminded of this at the age of 17. I was pulled over and asked to show my license. I reached to get it from the glove box, and noticed the officer step back and unsnap[1] his gun holster[2]. I froze. I remembered "The Talk." I survived.

Once a Black child learns this truth, that knowledge marks the early end of their childhood. I remember my parents schooling me on all that my white friends could do with no real consequence, and how the same things could get me killed. Once I processed this, I understood the reality that the world has different rules for Black people, that the people who wear police uniforms get to play by different rules. I understood that the American ideal is only ever ideal for white people.

For me, "The Talk" was not a singular event, but a series of conversations that began when I was about 10. The content of those talks surely impacted me, but never more than when I saw the hint of a tear or fear in my dad's eye. To me, his fear meant that beyond this point he could not protect me.

That was when I remember becoming aware that the world was not as safe for me as it was for my white friends. Taking safety for granted was beginning to slip between my fingers.

Recently I wondered, what would happen if every white child's parent sat him or her down for "The Talk"? It could be the same talk Black children get, with one difference: They'd be told that if they forget, if they ask the officer a question or even if they get angry, there may (or may not) be a consequence. But, because of their whiteness, the consequence would almost never be death. The parent would explain how white privilege[3] wraps their white child in love, protects them from the harsh condemnation[4] of prejudice and protects their childhood well into their teens and early 20s.

I've read research that shows that 63% of white adults believe Blacks are treated less advantageous than whites by the criminal justice system; and that 84% of Black adults believe Blacks are treated less advantageous. Do white people ever wonder why a full 21% more Black people believe this? So many white people claim to be offended by Colin Kaepernick taking a knee to protest police brutality. Do they want to watch Black athletes play ball without having to think about their humanity, without having to think about them driving home from the stadium – driving while Black in an expensive car, which is a "suspicious[5] situation" and could easily become dangerous? I wonder if they don't want to think about what would happen when an officer would feel threatened by a large Black man, maybe larger than George Floyd, who might have a weapon or who might forget the things his parents told him long ago, when they sat him down for "The Talk."

As nations go, America is a child. Someone needs to be the parent and sit America down for "The Talk." The difference between Black and white in America is as clear as the difference between "thuggish behavior" and "youthful indiscretion[6]," as clear as the difference between "known gang member" and "young person with a bright future," as clear as the difference between Tamir Rice and Dylann Roof.

Tamir was a 12-year-old Black child playing in a park. Those sworn to serve and protect Tamir drove up and immediately shot him dead. Dylann was a 21-year-old white man. He entered a church and shot a group of Black Bible-worshipers, killing nine of them. Those sworn to serve and protect Dylann arrested him the next day. Police took him alive. He was hungry, so the officers bought him a Burger King meal.

America is a young person with a bright future. America is a thug. America is no stranger to youthful indiscretion. America is a known gang member. No one has ever sat America down for "The Talk." Isn't it time someone did?

David W. Janey, WBUR, 2021 (adapted)

1 to unsnap [ʌn'snæp] lösen ○ **2** holster ['həʊlstə] Halfter ○ **3** white privilege = an advantage given to white people ○
4 condemnation [ˌkɒndem'neɪʃən] Verurteilung ○ **5** suspicious [sə'spɪʃəs] verdächtig ○ **6** indiscretion [ˌɪndɪ'skreʃən] Fehltritt

b) *Complete the sentences.*

1. In Black families, "The Talk" is about when parents teach their children how to behave when the police would pull them over.
2. Having "The Talk" is critical for Black people because their life could depend on it.
3. The author's childhood ended early when he understood that the Talk was important and real! When he was 17 he was pulled over and asked to show his license. The officer was ready to pull out his gun! That was traumatizing
4. Giving white children "The Talk" would teach them that even if they'd do anything illegal, they'd never experience the same consequences as a black person

c) *Underline the correct answers. Sometimes more than one answer can be correct.*

1. Research shows that **84 % of Black people believe Black people are treated worse than white people | 21 % of white people wonder why Black people are treated worse | nearly two out of three white adults agree that white people have an advantage** in the criminal justice system.
2. Black athletes **have been criticised for protesting police brutality at sports events. | think about their safety during games. | protesting forces white people think about the reality of being Black in America.**
3. Driving while Black **means Black people need to be careful drivers. | can be enough to make police officers suspicious. | in an expensive car can lead to trouble for Black people.**

d) *Answer these questions in your exercise book. Take notes.*

1. Explain what is being expressed with the opposites "thuggish behavior" versus "youthful indiscretion", "known gang member" versus "young person with a bright future", and Tamir Rice versus Dylann Roof (ll. 77–81).
2. Explain why the author believes someone should have "The Talk" with America.

WRITING **19**

Fearing the police

→ SB 57/1; S7–10, S17

*Choose **one** of these tasks and write about 200 words in your exercise book.*

1. Write a comment for a newspaper and explain why 'WWB' or 'DWB[1]' (Walking / Driving While Black) is often checked by police in the US. Say which steps could be taken to change this.
2. Describe and analyse the cartoon.

1 DWB *Wortspiel mit DWI (driving while intoxicated = Alkohol / Drogen am Steuer), Anspielung auf häufigere Verkehrskontrollen bei African-Americans*

LANGUAGE **20**

Find the mistakes: A famous dress → SB 57/1

Read an article from a brochure by the Smithsonian National Museums. Decide if the underlined phrases are correct or not. Correct the mistakes.

At the Smithsonian National Museum of African American History & Culture, you (1) are finding many unusual objects on display. These range from letters (2) wrote during the American Revolution to electronics (3) using from early hip hop stars, from 16th century jewellery to today's clothes. One dress on display (4) was worned by Carlotta Walls on her first day of school at Little Rock Central High School in 1957. Carlotta was (5) one of nine African-American students to attend the (6) previous all-white school. Her uncle had told her that what (7) she will do was a once-in-a-lifetime event and that (8) she'd need a store-bought dress for the (9) ocassion. Even if Carlotta (10) knew that her dress would one day (11) to be display in a museum, she (12) couldn't have choosen a better one. The dress is black with blue letters – the perfect pattern for the first Black girl (13) attending the once-segregated school, for a (14) girl who loved learning and (15) was willing standing up to segregationists to get (16) better education possible. Although Carlotta said she (17) have wanted never be a hero, she and the other Black students (18) showed extremely courage on that first day and on (19) everyday that they (20) have walked through the school doors.

LANGUAGE **21**

Mixed bag: Beyond the superstar → SB 57/1

Complete this newspaper article about Beyoncé with the missing words or phrases.

Many people don't know that besides ____________ a successful singer and actress, Beyoncé is ____________ an activist. She ____________ several causes ____________ vegan and Black-owned businesses ____________ owners serve ________ role models and she ____________ college scholarships ________ young people in the Black community. In her music, she uses her voice ____________ for social ____________ and ____________ racism. Beyoncé ____________ songs against police ____________ as well. By ____________ about the beauty of ____________ Black, she promotes cultural pride and empowers women – just ____________ to "Freedom" or "Run the World (Girls)", for example. Additionally, ____________ families ____________ don't have enough money for food is close to her heart. Talking about why she was an activist, Beyoncé said that every woman ____________ step up and take the lead.

SPEAKING 22 Black experiences in the US → SB 57/1; S14, S17

a) ***Warm-up:*** *Together with a partner, talk about the following questions.*

1. What are examples of unfair treatment? Think of different contexts: school, family, society.
2. What are possible reactions to unfair treatment especially if it happens again and again?
3. What comes to your mind when you think about racism? Name at least three things or situations.

b) ***Monologue:*** *Describe the cartoon to your partner. Analyse the cartoon and comment on how the person in your cartoon handles racism.*

Partner A

"I agree that racism is terrible, and I sympathize with your struggles, but Jesus Christ Larry, do we really have to talk about it?"

Partner B

c) ***Dialogue:*** *The questions "What race/nationality are you?" and "But where are you really from?" are considered discriminating and rude. Together with your partner, discuss reasons why and who might be affected. Include the statements in your discussion.*

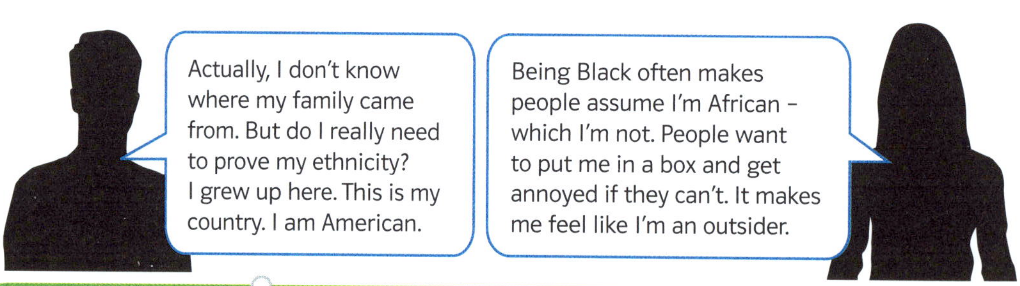

Useful phrases

I believe / feel / suppose … | It depends on … | … can / can't say a lot / anything / much about … | offensive / rude / racist / personal question | harmless / important / friendly question | … depends on the context / situation | It's not fair to say that … | Just because someone looks Black / Asian / wears a headscarf / … doesn't mean that … | You can't ignore that …

Self-assessment

On this page you can assess your performance. Look at the exercises in this workbook unit again and colour the traffic lights in the grid. Which skill(s) would you like to improve? The last column will tell you where to find help in your book.

Skill	Exercise(s)	Check	Help
LISTENING / VIEWING **I know how to ...** – understand the gist and the detail in listening texts and video clips (e.g. guided tour, interview, educational video).	5, 7 a)–d), 10	○ ○ ○	S13
READING **I know how to ...** – understand and analyse extracts from a novel.	3 a), d)–g)	○ ○ ○	S5–6, S11–12
– understand and analyse poems.	8	○ ○ ○	S5–6
– understand and analyse extracts from an autobiography.	17 a), d)–f)	○ ○ ○	S5–6
– understand and analyse newspaper articles.	18	○ ○ ○	S5–6, S11
SPEAKING **I know how to ...** – give a presentation.	3 h), 7 e)	○ ○ ○	S15
– present and discuss a meme or short video.	6	○ ○ ○	S15, S17, S19
– describe, analyse and discuss charts.	9	○ ○ ○	S18
– express my own feelings, experiences and ideas.	22 a)	○ ○ ○	S14
– describe, analyse and comment on cartoons.	22 b)	○ ○ ○	S17
– have a discussion with a partner.	22 c)	○ ○ ○	S14
WRITING **I know how to ...** – describe and analyse a cartoon.	2, 19	○ ○ ○	S17
– write a comment.	19	○ ○ ○	S7–10
MEDIATION **I know how to ...** – transfer relevant information into the target language in a way that is appropriate to the target audience and the situation.	13	○ ○ ○	S5, S16
MEDIA COMPETENCE **I know how to ...** – assess different (online) sources.	14, 15, 16	○ ○ ○	S3
VOCABULARY / GRAMMAR **I know how to ...** – use relevant vocabulary and appropriate grammar to talk and write about African-Americans in the US.	1, 4, 11, 12, 20, 21	○ ○ ○	S1–2
– deal with unknown words.	3 b)–c), 17 b)–c)	○ ○ ○	S1–2

Focus 4 Fight for your rights!

SPEAKING

1 Civil rights movement top ten

→ SB 62/5; S15, S21

Get together in a group and choose one of these ideas or your own. Create a poster and give a presentation on your topic.

10 civil rights movement activists everyone should know |
10 most **famous quotes** from the **civil rights movement** |
10 most **significant photos** from the **civil rights movement** |
10 most moving **civil rights movement monuments** |
10 myths about the **civil rights movement** |
10 places every **civil rights movement enthusiast** should visit |

Tip

Read through the criteria for good (online) resources again and make sure to double-check your facts.

VOCABULARY

2 The civil rights movement explained

→ SB 63/6

Complete this wiki text about the civil rights movement. Use synonyms (=), opposites (↔) or other related words (→) for the words in blue.

The US Civil Rights Movement (CRM) began in the late 1940s and ended in the late 1960s. It was a decades-long struggle for social ________________ (= fairness) for African-Americans. While Lincoln's Emancipation Proclamation and the Civil War officially ________________ (↔ to establish) slavery, they did not ensure equal ________________ (→ to treat) in everyday life. ________________ (↔ acceptance) against Black people continued not only, but especially, in the South. ________________ (→ racism) ideas influenced who could attend which schools, which jobs were available and even where people could live. The goals of the CRM were to stand up against racial ________________ (= unfair bias) and ________________ (= to ask for) equal rights. One of its best-known figures was Dr Martin Luther King, Jr., who believed that ________________ (= peaceful) ________________ (= demonstration) were the most effective way to fight against injustice. Even though racial ________________ (↔ integration) was made ________________ (↔ legal) by law, the goal of complete ________________ (→ equal) has not been reached. The struggle against an ________________ (→ to oppress) system continues to this day. The 21st century version of the CRM – Black Lives Matter – aims ________________ (= to bring) awareness of police ________________ (→ brutal) and racially motivated ________________ (= extreme force) against Black people. It is a ________________ (= involving ordinary people), all-inclusive movement, which was started by three African-American women.

MEDIATION

3 The duty to stand up against injustice

→ SB 63/8; S16

You and your friend Jasmine from the US are discussing different forms of protest. Use this article and write her an e-mail (about 180 words) in which you explain the role of civil disobedience for the civil rights movement and for the protests connected to the G20 summit in Hamburg in 2017. Also describe how right-wing groups misuse civil disobedience.

Martin Luther King und der zivile Ungehorsam

Martin Luther King war sich sicher: Die Mächtigen im Staat lassen sich nicht mit Argumenten überzeugen. Nur friedliches Aufbegehren gegen Unrecht könne einen Wandel herbeiführen.

Wann aber ist ein Gesetz ungerecht?
King hat sich in dieser Frage auf eindeutige Kriterien bezogen. Der Politikwissenschaftler Christian Volk paraphrasiert Kings Auffassung: „Ein ungerechtes Gesetz ist eins, das bei einer Gruppe Minderwertigkeitsgefühle hervorbringt, das Ungleichheiten zementiert, das die Seele zerstört, wie es die Rassengesetzgebung tut."

Aber bietet der parlamentarische Weg nicht genügend Möglichkeiten, Ungerechtigkeiten anzuklagen und auf Veränderung zu dringen?
Die Unterdrückungsgeschichte der schwarzen Bevölkerung sprach da eine andere Sprache. Auch Martin Luther King war zu einer eindeutigen Einschätzung gelangt, führt Volk aus: „King war davon überzeugt, dass er die Mächtigen im Staat nicht mit Argumenten überzeugen wird." Ziviler Ungehorsam hat deshalb die Aufgabe, „die Kosten in die Höhe zu treiben für die machthabende Gruppe, wenn diese am Status quo festhält." Die Kosten für den Erhalt des gesellschaftlichen Status quo in die Höhe treiben wollten auch die G20-Proteste in Hamburg im vergangenen Jahr. Dabei kam es teilweise zu brennenden Barrikaden und Ladenplünderungen. Anders als die schwarze Bürgerrechtsbewegung, zielten die Hamburger Gipfel-Proteste nicht auf konkrete rechtliche Veränderungen innerhalb der bestehenden Gesetzesrahmens, meint Volk. Ihre Ziele seien vielmehr mit der gegebenen gesellschaftlichen Ordnung nicht vereinbar: „Es geht im Grunde darum, dass die Konfrontation mit dem System gesucht wird, weil man sich nur in dieser Konfrontation dem Gehorsam, den das System von einem verlangt, verweigert." Bei den G20-Protesten hätte eine Gruppe infrage gestellt, wer in der aktuellen Politik überhaupt als legitimer Sprecher auftreten kann. „Diese Art von Protest verschiebt für einen kurzen Moment den Fokus auf jene, die möglicherweise bislang nicht auf diese Weise zur Sprache kommen." Gleichzeitig seien die Proteste von einer ungekannten Nüchternheit bestimmt: „Man weiß, dass man diese Ziele in absehbarer Zeit nicht realisiert bekommt. Das war für King völlig anders. King war der Überzeugung, dass die Verfassung der Vereinigten Staaten von Amerika erst vollständig realisiert ist, wenn die Rassentrennung aufgehoben ist und er war davon überzeugt, dass das zu schaffen ist. Bei den heutigen Protesten gegen den Kapitalismus sieht das ganz anders aus."

Ist rechter Protest auch ziviler Ungehorsam?
Mit größerem Optimismus machen sich aktuell auch rechte Gruppierungen, wie etwa die Identitären, Praktiken des zivilen Ungehorsams zu eigen. Volk meint, Protestaktionen der Identitären könne man – die Konzepte von Martin Luther King zugrunde gelegt – nicht als zivilen Ungehorsam auffassen: „Das hängt damit zusammen, dass ziviler Ungehorsam für King immer emanzipatorischer Natur ist. Die Idee dahinter ist, dass man den Kreis derer erweitert, die in den Genuss der Versprechen der Demokratie kommen. Und was wir im rechten, identitären Protest sehen, ist, dass man den Kreis jener einschränken möchte, die in den Genuss der demokratischen Versprechen kommen, nämlich auf weiße, meist nicht-muslimische und auch nicht-linke Bürgerinnen und Bürger." Eine weitere zentrale Abweichung rechter Proteste von den Motiven zivilen Ungehorsams in der Tradition von King macht Christian Volk in der Idee der Proteste als gelebte Praxis aus: „Die rechten, populistischen Bewegungen sagen im Grunde: Du kannst bleiben, wie du bist; die Welt um dich herum muss sich ändern. Auch für King muss die Welt um uns herum natürlich geändert werden, aber auch wir dürfen nicht von unserem Hass und unserer Frustration getrieben werden, wenn wir protestieren."

Christian Möller, Deutschlandfunk Kultur, 2018 (adaptiert)

READING

1 Another example of an influential musical genre → SB 64/2

a) *Read through the reference article and do the exercises.*

Spirituals

1 The millions of enslaved people who were taken from Africa to the Americas and the Caribbean islands brought with them the cultures and traditions of their homelands. In what became the southern states of the USA, generations of enslaved people combined the musical traditions of their ancestors with their experiences of slavery. This developed into a type of music known as spirituals, African-American spirituals, slave songs and African-American work songs. Spirituals were sung while the enslaved people were working, for leisure, for religious reasons and even to pass on secret messages about escaping from slavery. Spirituals were originally for a solo voice or were 'call and response', with one line sung by a single voice, followed by a line sung by everybody else in the group.

2 Slavery finally ended in all of the US with the end of the Civil War in 1865. Soon after that, touring groups began to perform spirituals to audiences around the country and abroad, and the spirituals musical tradition became better known. It also started to be adapted into new forms: blues (which developed in the southern states of the US in the 1860s), jazz and Black gospel music (sung in churches, and also known simply as gospel). These became the foundations for African-American music, which has been hugely influential in the development of Western pop music in general. The music that came out of the extreme cruelty and terrible living conditions suffered by the US enslaved people went on to transform pop music for the whole world.

3 Spirituals in their traditional form continue to be appreciated by present-day audiences. The Fisk Jubilee Singers gave their first concert in 1871 and the latest version of the group is still performing today. Early recordings of spirituals have featured in modern electronic music such as *Play*, a 1999 album by Moby, which sold more than 12 million copies.

Artist profile: Wallace Willis
Wallace Willis was an enslaved person in Oklahoma, USA in the mid-19th century. Like many enslaved people, Wallace and his wife 'Aunt Minerva' sang while they were working in their owner's cotton fields. He composed several 'plantation songs' which later became famous spirituals.
Key tracks: "Steal Away to Jesus" (around 1862), "Swing Low, Sweet Chariot" (after 1865)

b) *Find suitable headings for the paragraphs 1–3.*

1. ______________________

2. ______________________

3. ______________________

Enslaved people on a plantation in South Carolina, USA, 1862

c) *Underline the characteristics of spirituals in the text. Then listen to the song "Swing Low, Sweet Chariot" sung by the Fisk Jubilee Singers (1909) online and say in which way it is characteristic for spirituals.*

WRITING

2 Time line of pop songs → SB 65/3; S3, S7–10

a) *With a partner, choose a song that was important in pop music history. Create a poster with visuals, relevant facts (e.g. artist, genre, date) and a short text (about 80 words) on why the song was important.*

b) *Bring together your posters to create a time line of important pop songs and do a gallery walk.*

Focus 5 My generation?

WRITING

1 Mind the gap

→ SB 66/1; S17

Follow these steps and write a short text (about 120 words) about the cartoon by Steve Greenberg.

1. Describe and analyse the cartoon.
2. Relate the cartoon to your experience. Do older generations judge the music you listen to? How do you judge people based on the music they like?

VOCABULARY

2 Being part of something

→ SB 67/4

Alaska and Brayden explain why they are part of a subculture. Complete their personal profiles.

Alaska: "I became a hippie in the sixties because I didn't want to ____________ in with my ________________ parents' restrictive ideas on how I should live my ____________. They wanted me to ________________ the traditional path – ____________ married, start a ________________, have a successful ________________ as either a lawyer or doctor. I didn't want any of that! Instead, I wanted to take some ____________ and ____________ a bit of fun. Also, I shared the ________________ of the movement: anti-war, sexual freedom and, of course, love."

Brayden: "I was ________________ about gaming from an early age. It's always been my ________________ to get good at it, and I like the feeling of ________________ you get as part of the gaming community. I'm lucky that my parents are ________________ and willing to consider different ideas on how teenagers choose to ______________ their free time. They would never tell me gaming was a waste of ______________. Plus, it isn't my only hobby. I really enjoy ______________ out new things, too!"

1 contempt [kən'tempt] Verachtung ○ 2 to sob [sɒb] schluchzen

Unit 3 Youth (and) culture

VOCABULARY

1 Changing the game → SB 68/1

Complete this article about how video gaming is changing society.

Often people who don't ________________ with gaming culture like to put the label of "nerdy" on it. But, in fact, gaming has been part of global m________________ culture for years. Today, the video gaming ________________ makes big money, ________________ an estimated 160 billion US dollars in 2020. Being a multi-billion-dollar business with a growing ____________ of players, it has undeniably left its ______________ on society.

Gaming has had a significant _______________ on how people, especially young people, socialise[1]. Gamers do not just ______________ online to play, but to ______________ up with friends. They can c________________ with people from ________________ the word. Although people's backgrounds may _______________, the players all share the same ____________ of purpose and an enthusiasm for the game. Moreover, gaming is changing our educational system by ______________ outdated ways of teaching and __________________ motivating opportunities for learning instead. Gaming helps students ____________ from failure, e________________ creativity and im________________ students' problem-solving ________________ – qualities needed in future workers.

As the video gaming industry ______________ to grow, it is set to ________________ an even greater impression on our society in the future.

SPEAKING

2 What would you spend it on? → SB 68/1; S14

a) *Read the text about Italy's culture bonus and with a partner discuss what you would spend it on.*

In 2016, the Italian government introduced a cultural bonus of 500 Euro for all 18-year-olds. The government wanted to invest in the future of young people and enable them to be part of the country's cultural and social life. The teenagers can spend this money on certain categories which include books, cinema, theatre and dance, music and concerts, cultural events, museums, monuments and parks, newspaper subscriptions[2] and music, theatre or foreign language classes.

b) *Do a survey to find out about how different age groups would spend the culture bonus. Present and analyse your results.*

1 to socialise ['səʊʃlaɪz] Kontakte pflegen ○ 2 subscription [səb'skrɪpʃn] Abonnement

LISTENING

3 Talking about generations → SB 70/1; S13

A 13-15

a) *Listen to the complete interview with Dr Rose Barns, a sociologist researching generations and their characteristics. Match the generations to the words and phrases that describe them best.*

1. Baby Boomers
2. Gen X
3. Gen Y / Millennials
4. Gen Z
5. Gen Alpha

a) confident, tolerant, curious
b) confident, innovative, action-oriented
c) global, digital, visual, independent
d) logical, independent, good at problem-solving
e) loyal, independent, like stability

b) *Listen to part 1 and answer these questions in your exercise book.*

1. How is 'generation' defined?
2. What influences the people in a generation?

c) *Listen to parts 2 and 3. Copy and complete the grid in your exercise book.*

generation	years	attitude to technology	attitude to work
Baby boomers	1946 – …		
Gen X			
Gen Y / Millennials			
Gen Z		interested in virtual and augmented reality	
Gen Alpha			

d) *Tick ✔ the general trends Dr Barns mentions.*

1. ☐ The level of education has improved, especially in girls and young women.
2. ☐ People have become more specialised in their field of study or work.
3. ☐ Experiences are becoming more important than material things.
4. ☐ The age at which people get married and start a family is increasing.
5. ☐ Previous generations spent more time working.

SPEAKING

4 A day in my life → SB 70/1; S15, S19

a) *Create a 60-second video which shows a typical day in your life. Include audio (music and / or speech) and write a short caption for your video.*

b) *Present your video and comment on why it does or doesn't show a typical day for teenagers from your generation, which elements of youth culture are included (e.g. fashion, music, technology) and how they are representative of your generation and / or the subculture you belong to.*

c) *In small groups, research and find out how a typical day looks for teenagers in other countries. Discuss how your days are similar or different.*

Tip
Make sure to check for copyright before using any materials that aren't your own.

WRITING

5 Analysing a teen movie trailer → SB 73/2; S8–11, S19

a) *Movie trailers are advertisements for new movies. A trailer typically includes a preview of the plot, presents the main characters and gives further important information (e.g. director, release date). Choose one of these or any other teen movie and watch the trailer for the movie online.*

The Breakfast Club (1985) | 10 things I hate about you (1999) | Save the Last Dance (2001) | Love, Simon (2018)

b) *Write an analysis of the trailer (about 200 words) in your exercise book. In the conclusion, give your opinion on the movie trailer.*

Analysing a movie trailer
- genre (e.g. horror, musical), important information (e.g. studio, director, actors), date, target audience
- characters, plot
- how it is made and which effect / purpose this has
  - visuals: scenes shown, text cards, editing
  - audio: music, sound effects, voiceover

READING

6 Online friendships → SB 73/2; S4–6, S10–11

a) *Read this article about online friendships and do the exercises.*

Online friendships – real or fake?

The internet can be a great place for both people with good and bad intentions. But because of the latter, online friends are often misjudged as creeps[1] or fakes. But with that mindset you miss out on the other half – the honest and open-minded people whom you could form a long-lasting friendship with.

But what exactly is friendship? Well, according to Aristotle, there are three types of friendships: friendships of utility[2], pleasure, and virtue[3]. Friendships of utility happen "by accident" and are not permanent at all. Both people get some sort of benefit from the exchange, but there is no intimate connection. Then there are friendships based on pleasure, also known as a shared interest. They end once that interest changes. The most long-lasting, most intimate, and most "complete" form of friendship is the one that is based on the appreciation of each other's virtues. These friendships take time to form, and you go through ups and downs together.

Sure, the internet did not exist 2,000 years ago, but I am convinced that Aristotle would have come to the same conclusions about friendship if he had chatted to people online.

So, if the types of friendships we can make online and offline are the same and we assume that both are based on mutual goodwill[4] (something essential according to Aristotle), why do we still label online friendships as fake or dubious?

Actually, online friendships are even better than offline friendships in some ways. I am Asian-American, queer, and socially awkward. Online no one knows who I am. That means that I face a lot less prejudices. People do not judge me for my race, the way I look or for liking T-shirts with funny slogans.

When you belong to a minority group, you will not only find less prejudice, but (often) also much more support online. I have met one of my best friends online through a queer support group. Even though we live hundreds of kilometres apart, they are essential for my mental well-being because I can talk to them about what it means to be queer in a small town in the Midwest – something my non-queer friends wouldn't understand. We have supported each other through some tough times and talk or video chat on an almost daily basis.

1 creep [kriːp] widerlicher Typ ○ **2** utility [juːˈtɪləti] Nutzen ○ **3** virtue [ˈvɜːtʃuː] Tugend ○ **4** goodwill [gʊdˈwɪl] Wohlwollen

Also, it can be hard for me to start a conversation in real life because I feel awkward or judged. Initiating a conversation online feels a lot safer. I can think about what I want to write, and I can leave a conversation whenever I want. Talking to strangers on the internet has also helped me improve my social skills. I now know how to get from a meaningless "hey what's up?" – "nothing much. u?" exchange of words to having an actual conversation.

Last but not least, I can find people with the same interests and hobbies online. People who agree Pokémon is cool and who share my love for Minecraft. Plus, meeting people with the same interests from around the world can add cultural perspectives and allows for deeper conversations.

All in all, I would say that the quality of an online friendship depends on yourself and your intentions, commitment and openness towards the other person. In conclusion, online friendships should not be quickly judged and thus labelled as fake or "not real" but need to be evaluated individually.

Daya Davis, Student Magazine, 2022

b) *Complete these tasks in your exercise book:*

1. In your own words, define the types of friendship according to Aristotle and give an example for each.
2. Name the benefits of online friendships according to the author.

c) *In your exercise book, analyse the perspective of the article and how this is connected to the purpose and style of the article.*

d) *Choose two arguments made about online friendships in the article and compare them to your own experiences. Discuss them with a partner.*

LANGUAGE

7 Error spotting: Subculture sports in the Olympics → SB 73/2

Read the short article on subculture sports in the Olympics and decide if the underlined words and phrases are correct or not. Correct the mistakes.

The popularity of the Olympic Games (1) has been declining over the years, (2) particular among the younger generation. This is one reason (3) because the International Olympic Committee (IOC) (4) start to introduce sports that (5) could attract the interest of younger viewers. Over the last 30 years, new sports, such as snowboarding, BMX racing and skateboarding (6) are already be adopt into the Olympics and breakdancing (7) will make its debut in the Paris Olympics in 2024.

However, (8) these are not (9) well news for everyone (10) be involved. Many enthusiasts of these sports feel that their subcultures (11) is being controlled and redesigned by the rules and formats of the (12) powerfully IOC. Native Hawaiians criticise that surfing is even further (13) culturaly apropriated by this multi-billion-dollar industry, climbers claim that speed climbing is not in line with (14) the climbing philosophy and break dancers wonder if the free spirit of breakdancing (15) can actually be brought into such a strongly regulated context like the Olympics or if it (16) is unavoidable that the things (17), which make the sport so unique will be lost.

But, of course, (18) becoming an Olympic sport also has (19) it's benefits. When a new sport (20) adopts by the IOC, it also (21) gain access to funding and will be recognised internationally.

VIEWING

8 Hip hop in education

→ SB 75/1; S19

V5

a) *Listen to the talk by Dr Christopher Emdin about hip hop in education. Complete the text.*

According to Dr Emdin, hip hop is representative of the ______________________________ of young people of color. It was originally created in ________________________ by young people of color who didn't ______________________ and, at first, it was only considered a trend which wouldn't last for long. However, hip hop has become a ______________________ phenomenon and is considered a great ________________________ artifact today.

b) *Name five elements of hip hop that Dr Emdin mentions.*

____

____

c) *Tick ✔ the correct answer. Dr Emdin believes that hip hop can play an important role in the classroom because …*

1. ☐ students can learn how to rap, breakdance and create graffiti.
2. ☐ the music helps students to concentrate.
3. ☐ it includes many different elements that students can relate to.
4. ☐ students can express their feelings through music.

d) *Give three examples of what Dr Emdin achieved or wants to achieve with his project "Science Genius".*

____

____

____

____

____

e) *Dr Emdin compares Galileo to NWA **(A)** and Albert Einstein to Jay-Z **(B)**. Match the pairs to the evidence he gives to support his comparisons. There are two extra.*

1. ☐ By acknowledging the things around them, they proved that they mattered.
2. ☐ Both wanted people to understand the good things that matter in life.
3. ☐ Both were brilliant and had musical talent.
4. ☐ By combining scientific and musical skills, they were able to understand their environment better.
5. ☐ By taking things out of their usual environment and analysing them closely, they were able to create something more complex.

MEDIATION

9 Materialism and hip hop → SB 76/2; S16

Your friend Parveen from Canada is a big hip hop fan. However, she asks herself why hip hop is often about status and material things. Use the interview to write her an e-mail (about 170 words) in which you explain why there is a lot of materialism in hip hop and why there are a lot of hip hop artists who succeeded in business.

Warum Hip-Hop gut zur Wirtschaft passt

"Der Wille zum Erfolg ist in der DNA der Hip-Hop-Kultur fest verankert", sagt der Unternehmensberater Tobias Kargoll. Im DW-Gespräch erklärt er, warum das Underdog-Mindset als Businessfaktor so erfolgreich ist.

DW: In Ihrem neuen Buch "Erfolgsformel Hip-Hop" heißt es, dass sich fast die Hälfte der Generation Z mit dieser Kultur identifiziert. Auch die Zusammenarbeit von Wirtschaftsunternehmen und Konzernen außerhalb der Musikbranche mit Künstlern aus dem Hip-Hop Bereich erreicht immer neue Dimensionen. Welche Beispiele fallen Ihnen spontan ein?

Tobias Kargoll: Es gab und gibt natürlich in 50 Jahren Hip-Hop eine Menge aufsehenerregende Themen: Beispielsweise wurde Kanye West mit seinem Sneaker-Brand Yeezy zum Milliardär. Der Rapper Jay-Z gründete 1999 das Streetwear-Label Rocawear und stieß es 2007 für 200 Millionen US-Dollar wieder ab. Am erfolgreichsten als Geschäftsmann ist wohl der Rapper Dr. Dre, dessen Kopfhörer-Hersteller Beats Electronics 2014 für 3,2 Milliarden US-Dollar von Apple übernommen wurde.

Warum bringt ausgerechnet diese Subkultur so viele erfolgreiche Unternehmer hervor?

Das Potenzial liegt darin, dass Hip-Hop eine sehr markenaffine Kultur ist. Man kommuniziert auch über Marken und Produkte. Hip-Hop ist das Kind einer kapitalistischen Gesellschaft, geboren in den 1970er Jahren in armen New Yorker Stadtteilen wie der Bronx oder Queens. Wer dort lebte – häufig Puerto Ricaner oder Afroamerikaner – hatte den Reichtum von Manhattan ständig vor Augen und war doch davon ausgeschlossen. Hip-Hop hat viel mit dem Glauben an Selbstwirksamkeit zu tun. Man möchte sichtbar werden, sich selbst ausdrücken und all das erreichen, was einem die Gesellschaft vorenthalten will. Dazu gehört auch sozialer Aufstieg. Wer es allen Hindernissen zum Trotz vom Tellerwäscher zum Millionär schafft, der nutzt Statussymbole als Trophäe für das Erreichte.

In Ihrem Buch beschreiben Sie das konkrete Mindset, also die bestimmten Denkweisen der Hip-Hop-Künstler, die zum geschäftlichen Erfolg führen. Wie sehen diese Techniken aus?

Der Wille zum Erfolg ist ganz tief in der Hip-Hop-Kultur verankert: Der Underdog-Mindset, es aus ärmlichen, begrenzten Verhältnissen gegen alle Widerstände nach ganz oben schaffen zu wollen. Außerdem ist der Wettbewerbsgedanke ein prägendes Element. Denken Sie an die Rap- oder Dance-Battles, bei denen sich die Konkurrenten gegenseitig übertrumpfen. Außerdem spielt Kollaboration im Hip-Hop eine wichtige Rolle. Solokünstler versammeln ihre eigene Crew hinter sich, arbeiten auch projektbezogen mit anderen Künstlern zusammen, quasi um Synergieeffekte zu erzeugen, wie man im Management-Jargon sagen würde.

Sie meinen, die Hip-Hop-Szene ist eine Art Spiegel der kapitalistischen Welt – nur unter anderen Vorzeichen? Wenn man kein Geld hat, muss man improvisieren und neue Wege finden, um zu erreichen, was man haben will?

Das findet man schon genauso bei den ersten Hip-Hop-Partys, wo sich Leute ihre Boxen aus Ölfässern gebaut haben und sich an den Autowracks, die in New York in den Straßen standen, bedient haben, um sich ihre Technik zusammenzubasteln. Man findet selbst Wege, um im System zu existieren. Das ist ein wichtiger Schlüssel zum Erfolg von Hip-Hop Kultur. Der eigene Erfolg ist ein kleiner Sieg über das System und daran lässt man sein direktes Umfeld teilhaben. Das ist die Haltung, die in Verbindung mit einer Menge Kreativität oft zu unerwarteten Erfolgen von Underdogs führt, denen am Anfang die Mittel gefehlt haben.

Klaus Ulrich, Deutsche Welle, 2021 (adaptiert)

READING **10**

A song analysis

→ SB 77/3; S4–7, S10–11

a) *Queen Latifah is a hip hop artist, actress, talk show host and a film producer. Her song* U.N.I.T.Y *won her a Grammy Award in 1995, and she was the first hip hop artist to receive a star on the Hollywood Walk of Fame. Read the lyrics to* U.N.I.T.Y *and do the exercises.*

Uh, U.N.I.T.Y., U.N.I.T.Y. that's a unity
U.N.I.T.Y., love a black man from
infinity to infinity
(Who you calling a bitch[1]?)
U.N.I.T.Y., U.N.I.T.Y. that's a unity
(You gotta let him know)
(You go, come on here we go)
U.N.I.T.Y., love a black woman from
(You got to let him know)
infinity to infinity
(You ain't a bitch or a ho[2])
U.N.I.T.Y., U.N.I.T.Y. that's a unity
(You gotta let him know)
(You go, come on here we go)
U.N.I.T.Y., love a black man from
(You got to let him know)
infinity to infinity
(You ain't a bitch or a ho)
Instinct leads me to another flow
Everytime I hear a brother call a girl a bitch or a ho
Trying to make a sister feel low
You know all of that gots to go
Now everybody knows there's exceptions to this rule
Now don't be getting mad, when we playing, it's cool
But don't you be calling out my name
I bring wrath to those who disrespect me like a dame
That's why I'm talking, one day I was walking down the block
I had my cutoff shorts on right cause it was crazy hot
I walked past these dudes when they passed me
One of 'em felt my booty[3], he was nasty
I turned around red, somebody was catching the wrath
Then the little one said (Yeah me bitch) and laughed
Since he was with his boys he tried to break fly
Huh, I punched him dead in his eye and said "Who you calling a bitch?"

Words: Queen Latifah, Kier "Kay Gee" Gist (adapted)

b) *Find the words and phrases in the text for these definitions.*

1. the state of being in agreement and working together: ____________________
2. the state of having no end: ____________________
3. extreme anger: ____________________
4. to change one's behaviour to impress others: ____________________

c) *Tick ✔ which issues are addressed in the song. Underline the main one.*

1. ☐ sexism
2. ☐ catcalling[4]
3. ☐ inappropriate clothing
4. ☐ disrespectful language
5. ☐ brother sister rivalry
6. ☐ harassment[5]

d) *Complete these exercises in your exercise book:*

1. In the chorus the word "unity" is repeated frequently. Explain who Queen Latifah wants to see united and why.
2. Explain which "exception to this rule" (l. 23) Queen Latifah makes.
3. Comment on if the main issue is an issue of society in general or hip hop culture specifically, and if it's still relevant today.

SPEAKING

e) *In the US curse words often get censored when a song is played by a radio or TV station, however, many stations didn't take out the curse words when playing* U.N.I.T.Y. *Discuss why you think they didn't.*

1 bitch *(sl)* ['bɪtʃ] *Schimpfwort für Frauen* ○ 2 ho *(sl)* [həʊ] *Schimpfwort für Frauen* ○ 3 booty *(sl)* [bu:ti] Po ○
4 catcalling ['kætkɔ:lɪŋ] *sexuell anzügliches Rufen im öffentlichen Raum* ○ 5 harassment [hə'ræsmənt] Belästigung

LANGUAGE

11 Mixed bag: A chat before class starts → SB 77/3

Ella and Dan are talking about hip hop before their music class. Complete the dialogue.

Ella: I really wish Mr Stevens ________________ (not) asked us to discuss hip hop ________ class.

Dan: Why? We ___________________________ to a lot of great hip hop artists recently.

Ella: I like the energy of hip hop. If only the artists _______________________ (not) about violence and sex all the time. I'm tired of _____________________ yet another rapper – male and _____________ – bring ________ guns in their songs or how after _____________ successful everyone d_____________ them now.

Dan: They only ________________ about ___________ experiences in life. Many ___________ from poor urban areas and if violence and guns hadn't been an actual part of their lives, they ___________________ (not) included them in their lyrics. Also, _____________ of artists sing about how they _______________________ these struggles. I think that's inspiring!

Ella: But tell me ________ a lot of ________ women in the songs ___________________________ only as sexual objects. ________ a woman, I find the language _____________ hip hop artists use i_____________ and rude.

Dan: I get what you ______________________. But remember that Mr Stevens said that sexism ________ not only a problem in hip hop, but the music industry in _____________. You're right though that it is _______________________ bad in hip hop. Luckily, a lot of new female hip hop artists ___________________ these days. It's time for some more diversity in hip hop.

WRITING

12 The pros and cons of virtual concerts → SB 79/1; S8–10

Virtual concerts are becoming more and more popular. According to a worldwide survey, more than 70% of participants have watched a livestream concert or music event. Research online and write an argumentative essay (about 250 words) on the pros and cons of virtual concerts.

Tip

For the main body of your essay, there are two different structures you can follow:

- one side's arguments first, and then counter arguments (pro-pro-pro; con-con-con)
- argument and counter argument in the same paragraph (pro-con; pro-con; pro-con)

READING 13 Video game murder → SB 79/2; S5–6, S10–11

a) *Kiera Johnson is a seventeen-year-old teenager and one of the few Black students at her school. She is also the game developer of the secret online VR game,* SLAY *– a video game which is meant to be a safe space for the Black community worldwide. She is in the school cafeteria following the news on one of the TVs there when she gets to know about the murder of a fellow* SLAYer. *Read the novel excerpt and do the exercises.*

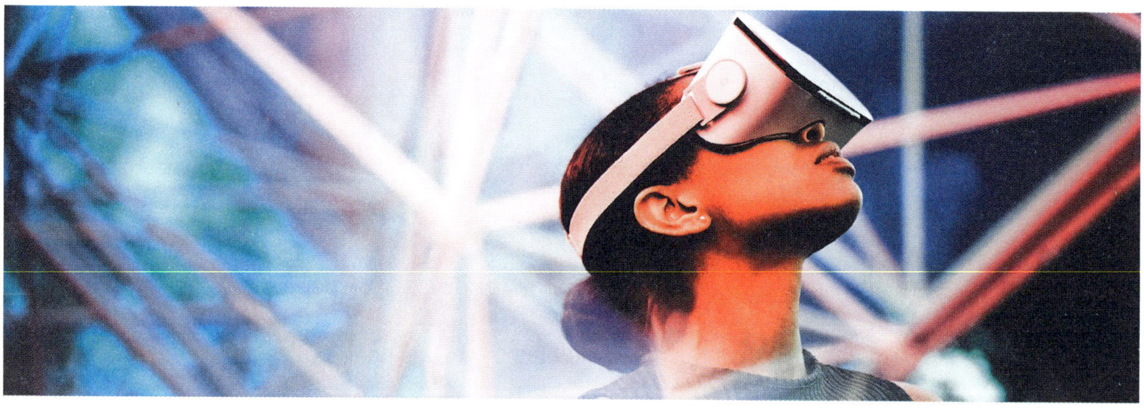

The banner now reads something new that strikes me.

Boy shot in his sleep over video game.

My chest tightens at the reminder of how cruel people can be. As a game developer, I'm not just an artist. I'm not just a coder. I feel a certain responsibility for the people who play my game. Their characters are an extension[1] of them, after all. There are real people behind those characters, and I suddenly feel sorry for whoever developed the game behind this murder. I watch and wait to see which game it is, although I suspect it's *Legacy of Planets*, that MMORPG[2] Wyatt always plays. That game has millions of players, some of whom have died of pulmonary embolisms[3] from blood clots[4] that can develop after sitting still and doing nothing but playing for days in a row. With how serious people take *Legacy,* I wouldn't be surprised to hear of someone being killed in real life over it.

As I'm staring up at the TV, the closed-captioning appears below a boy who looks a few years younger than me, tears streaming down his face.

It was over a damn game, man. It was a game! That's my brother in there.

And what game is that? asks the reporter.

S'called SLAY. *Homeboy, Jamal, and I been playing every night for forever.*

The words freeze me where I sit, and I read them again to make sure I'm not imagining it. SLAY. My mind can't process the words. It takes me a moment to realize and I suddenly feel like throwing up.

We ran a hustle together. We spent hours SLAYing, *dueling, stacking coins. We put all our coins in Jamal's account so he could buy stuff for us. He tried to hold 'em for ransom[5] for real dollars, and … this dude we never shoulda been playing with, he's bad news, man. Came and shot Jamal. He shot Jamal in his sleep for hijacking[6] damn game coins, man! That was my brother!*

It all washes over me so fast. I navigate through the swarms of students and disappear down the hallway to the bathroom, where I shut myself inside and try my best to breathe.

Kiera decides to skip class for the rest of the day and go home to log into SLAY.

Does this make me a murderer? Did I kill Jamal?

I've been staring at my VR screen so long my eyes are dry. My back and feet hurt from standing for too long. My hands are sweaty inside my gloves.

Anubis is standing in front of me. I found him in the Desert, exactly where his human – Jamal – left him. He's moving slightly, swaying slowly from side to side as if he's real.

Have I killed him? Was it me? It feels so painfully real now to remember there are actual people behind the characters I see in my headset. This Egyptian god of a character that stands before me, who's an epic warrior here in

1 extension [ɪk'stenʃn] Erweiterung ○ **2** MMORPG = Massively Multiplayer Online Role-Playing Game ○ **3** pulmonary embolism [ˌpʊlmənri 'embəlɪzm] Lungenembolie ○ **4** blood clot ['blʌd klɒt] Blutgerinnsel ○ **5** ransom ['rænsm] Lösegeld ○ **6** to hijack ['haɪdʒæk] klauen the *SLAY* universe, is just a kid in the real word – around my age. *Was* a kid. I can't stop shaking. This is my fault. I should've been more careful. I should've included in the list of game rules that you can't trade real money for *SLAY* coins. Not like it would've done anything. People do what people do. But … I can't shake this feeling, that I could've done *something*.

I think back to that day I came home from Harper's house three years ago, when we both played *Legacy of Planets* – it was the very first time I was called a n*****. After I had finally customized my character, who had to be a dwarf if I wanted to make her skin as dark as mine is in real life, I went to the first character I saw on the map – I don't even remember his username – and he took one look at my character and whipped out that word. I never told Harper or Wyatt because I didn't want to ruin the game for them. In fact, I kept playing. I wanted so badly to love *Legacy of Planets*, because who doesn't love the idea of having a virtual miniature them who can go on campaigns and fight dragons with no risks except for virtual character damage and loss of coins? Who doesn't want to have a world at their fingertips – where you can do whatever you want within the limits of the game, where your actions have no consequences, and where you can hide behind a keyboard without being held responsible for what you say or do? Everyone wants that freedom. And whenever I played *Legacy*, I'd hear all the things people wish they could say to people in real life.

I remember creating Emerald, making her skin my shade, just a few shades shy of passing the paper bag test, wondering how I could share her with everyone I knew who needed a world like this. I never thought the game would get this big, this time-consuming, or this dangerous. I never thought a boy would lose his life because of me. I stare at Anubis, still swaying slightly, looking silently at me. I hold out my hands and look down at them, at Emerald's hands. Would I still have created her if I had known?

From: Brittney Morris, *SLAY* (adapted)

b) *Find the words for these definitions in the text and mark them.*

1. display of text of the spoken part of a program | 2. way of making money | 3. build sth according to personal preferences | 4. small mythological manlike being | 5. degree of darkness or lightness of a colour

c) *Match these people or things with the correct description of them.*

1. *Legacy of Planets*
2. Wyatt and Harper
3. Jamal
4. Anubis
5. Emerald

a) boy who was murdered over game coins
b) Kiera's friends
c) Jamal's character in *SLAY*
d) Kiera's character in *SLAY*
e) popular online game

d) *In your exercise book, describe how Kiera's reaction and attitude changes when she realises the murder of Jamal is connected to* SLAY *and not to* Legacy of Planets.

e) *Copy the grid into your exercise book and complete it with information from the text. Give lines.*

advantages and possibilities of video games for developers and users	downsides and real-life consequences of video games for developers and users
– *video games as a form of art / creative expression (l. 6)* – …	– *responsibility of developer for negative impact of game on users (ll. 7–8)* – …

f) *With a partner discuss if you think Keira is responsible for what happened to Jamal.*

WRITING

g) *Choose* ***one*** *of these tasks and write about 200 words in your exercise book.*

1. Write a diary entry from Kiera's perspective about what happened.
2. Write a newspaper article about what happened.

READING **14**

Analysing social media posts → SB 80/3; S4–6

a) *Read these two fictional social media posts about sustainable living and do the exercises.*

Daisyflow

2h ago
Liked by **sustainabletony** and **6,237** others

In the US alone 50 billion single-use coffee cups are thrown away every year. That's why I've been using reusable coffee cups for almost three years now and you should too.

My latest fav is from @coffeecups. It fits one cup of coffee perfectly and keeps it hot for hours. Plus, they are using 100% recycled materials and produce their cups in the US. A must-have for all eco-friendly coffee lovers!

If you are looking for a stylish and functional reusable cup, use my discount code "daisyflow20" to get 20% off your first order.

sustainabletony

yesterday
389 likes

I had a lot of goals on my list for this new year – a lot of personal goals. However, I don't just want to make my own life better, so my main goal for this year is to live more sustainably. That means:

- going completely vegan
- not buying anything I do not absolutely need
- compensation of flight emissions
- starting a vertical garden on my balcony
- going completely paperless

We all know it's about time that we do better, so join me and let's save the world together.

b) *With a partner complete these exercises:*

1. Explain what the posts are about and how their message is similar but also contradicting.
2. Describe the pictures and say how they relate to the content of the post.
3. Discuss what the intentions of the posts could have been.
4. Research online if what the posts claim about sustainable living is true or not.

SPEAKING

c) *With a partner discuss other contradicting messages that you find online and how these might influence you. Use these ideas or your own.*

mental health awareness vs. productivity | body acceptance vs. fitness | authenticity vs. perfectionism

VOCABULARY **15**

Finding opposites → SB 81/4

a) *Find pairs of opposites and write them in your exercise book.*

active | artistic | colourful | confident | conservative | easy-going | fake | genuine | idle | matter-of-fact | pale | posh | radical | self-conscious | stiff | simple

b) *Match the adjectives from a) with a subculture and say why.*
Example: Skaters can be described as active because they are outside a lot.

SKILLS 16 Talking about social media → SB 83/1

Put these words and phrases about social media into the correct group. Add at least three words of your own to each group.

addiction | to comment | communication | cooperation | cyberbullying | entertainment | to feel overwhelmed | to follow | to get information | hate speech | to keep in touch | to like | marketing | oversharing | to post | pressure | privacy issues | to share | sharing | support | to tag | to waste time

functions	purposes	risks

SKILLS 17 Types of social media → SB 83/2

a) *Match the different types of social media with their main purpose.*

1. social networking
2. media sharing networks
3. consumer review networks
4. discussion forums
5. interest-based networks
6. sharing economy networks
7. bookmarking networks

a) to connect with people
b) to explore hobbies and interests
c) to read and write reviews
d) to save and organise content
e) to exchange knowledge, opinions and news
f) to share photos, videos, etc.
g) to share resources (e.g. goods, skills, services)

b) *With a partner discuss which types of social media you (don't) use and why (not).*

SKILLS 18 To post or not to post → SB 83/3

Look at these photos and with a partner discuss if posting them online is ok or not and on what this depends.

1 Class photo

2 Selfie with your best friends

3 Photo from your holiday in New York

4 Picture from a search engine

READING **19** ## Instapoetry

→ SB 85/1; S4–6, S10–11

a) *Rupi Kaur was born in India and immigrated to Canada with her parents at a young age. She is a poet, illustrator, photographer and author. She became famous through her poems on social media. Read these four poems by Rupi Kaur and do the exercises.*

A

i don't know what living a balanced life feels like
when i am sad
i don't cry i pour[1]
when i am happy
i don't smile i glow
when i am angry
i don't yell i burn

the good thing about feeling in extremes is
when i love i give them wings
but perhaps that isn't
such a good thing cause
they always tend to leave
and you should see me
when my heart is broken
i don't grieve[2]
i shatter[3]

B

if you were born with
the weakness to fall
you were born with
the strength to rise

C

trying to convince myself
i am allowed
to take up space
is like writing with
my left hand
when i was born
to use my right

– the idea of shrinking is hereditary[4]

D

i do not want to have you
to fill the empty parts of me
i want to be full of my own
i want to be so complete
i could light[5] a whole city
and then
i want to have you
cause the two of us combined
could set it on fire

Poems from: Rupi Kaur, *milk and honey*

b) *Rupi Kaur divided her book into four chapters which all deal with a different theme. Match the poems to the chapters they belong to. Give reasons.*

1. ☐ the hurting
2. ☐ the loving
3. ☐ the breaking
4. ☐ the healing

c) *Choose **one** of the poems and analyse it in your exercise book. Follow these steps:*

1. Explain what the poem is about and which topic(s) it deals with.
2. Analyse how the poem is structured. Does it follow the typical patterns of traditional poetry, or is it unusual? Think about stanzas, line breaks, rhythm, rhyme pattern and title.
3. Analyse the language of the poem. Think about word choice and literary devices.
4. Explain who the speaker is and whom they are speaking to.

d) *Most of Rupi Kaur's poems come with a drawing. Create or find a drawing that goes with the poem you chose in c). Explain the connection between the poem and the drawing.*

e) *Instagram poems are often criticised for being too simple and not having enough substance. With a partner discuss if poems like poem B can be called poetry.*

1 to pour [pɔː] schütten ○ **2** to grieve [griːf] trauern ○ **3** to shatter [ˈʃætə] zerbrechen ○ **4** hereditary [hɪˈredɪtri] erblich ○ **5** *to light [laɪt] erhellen

LISTENING **20**

Female fandom[1] → SB 86/1; S13

A 16

a) *Listen to this podcast about fangirls. Tick ✔ the adjectives that are often used in generalised statements about fangirls.*

1. ☐ real
2. ☐ lively
3. ☐ crazy
4. ☐ ordinary
5. ☐ obsessed[2]
6. ☐ hysterical

b) *Complete Ashley's definition of a fangirl.*

Person who shows ______________, ______________, ______________ and sometimes obsession for a ______________ (e.g. ______________) or ______________ (e.g. ______________) they admire.

c) *How does Ashley compare and contrast fangirls with football fans? Take notes.*

____

____

____

d) *Are these statements true or false? Tick ✔ the correct answer.*

	true	false
1. Extreme male fans are described as crazy and hysterical.	☐	☐
2. Society perceives male fandom as something that is based on a deeper, knowledge-based understanding of a subject.	☐	☐
3. Unlike for girls, society's standards for boys are not based on stereotypes.	☐	☐
4. Female fandom is mainly based on the physical appearance of a celebrity.	☐	☐

e) *Complete these sentences.*

1. Fangirls can be called experts in their field of research because ______________________________
2. Fangirls use fanart ______________________________
3. Because of their shared passion and understanding for each other, fangirls ______________________________
4. Fangirls have the power ______________________________

SPEAKING **21**

A presentation on a video game → SB 87/1; S15

Give a three-minute presentation on a famous video game or a video game you enjoy playing. Your presentation should include a short summary of how the game works, why it is so popular and/or why you like it and in what ways it reflects your generation's interests.

1 fandom [fændəm] Fangemeinschaft ○ **2** obsessed [əbˈsest] besessen

LISTENING **22**

Fashion in subcultures → SB 87/1, S13

A17

a) *Listen to the radio interview about fashion in different subcultures. Match the three subcultures to the correct photo. One photo is extra.*

e-boys and e-girls | Dark Academia | scene kids

1

2

3

4

1 ________________ 2 ________________ 3 ________________ 4 ________________

b) *Tick ✔ the correct answer. Sometimes more than one answer is correct.*

1. E-boys and e-girls …
   a) ☐ are internet sensations.
   b) ☐ are popular for posting videos.
   c) ☐ don't agree with gender stereotypes.

2. E-kids style means …
   a) ☐ wearing only black and white clothing.
   b) ☐ trying to look soft, cute and innocent.
   c) ☐ putting on make-up like anime characters.

c) *Complete the text.*

Dark Academia describes a culture focused on ______________________. Its members enjoy ______________________ and ______________________________________, preferably in ________________ and ______________________. Formal ____________, ________________ and ______________ in ____________ colours or tartan design made from ____________________________ are typical clothing in *Dark Academia*. Their fashion style also reflects their ________________ because it influences the way they act and feel.

d) *Take notes on the mentioned aspects of the scene culture.*

1. **fashion style:** ____
   ____
   ____

2. **intention behind style:** ____
   ____

3. **music:** ____
   ____

LANGUAGE 23 Find the mistakes: Body positivity → SB 87/1

Read Jay's blog entry about teenage body images. Decide if the underlined words and phrases are correct or not. Correct the mistakes.

I (1) used hating my face and body and I (2) constant telled myself that I (3) were fat and unattractive. Teens (4) spent an enormous amount of time (5) to scroll through other (6) peoples' life: We follow influencers, celebrities and, of course, our friends on social media and at some point, we (7) ask us why we can't look like them. Girls always (8) appear skinny and boys (9) are showed as muscular. Both boys' and girls' faces (10) are been redesigned to perfection. Of course, with so many editing apps around, these photos (11) are wide from realistic. The beauty standard we are so (12) desperately to achieve (13) is only leaving us with feelings of self-hate and depression. However, I (14) had luck: My family and friends (15) made me realise that it really wasn't worth (16) wasting my life trying to be (17) anyone I'm not. That I'm perfectly OK the way I am. I immediately (18) stopped to edit my photos. Now I (19) write this blog because I believe everyone, especially teenagers, should be celebrating their own individuality and identity instead of (20) try to fit in with a senseless ideal.

______
______
______
______
______
______
______
______
______
______
______

LANGUAGE 24 Mixed bag: Does hip hop deserve its often negative image? → SB 87/1

Complete this newspaper comment about the image of hip hop with the missing words or phrases.

If you talk to parents around the world about hip hop, you ______ (often) the same reactions: Adults ______ their eyes, ______ their shoulders and ______, "I just can't understand what ______ my kids listen to this *awful* music." ______ disrespect towards women, ______ the use of drugs and in general ______ a negative influence on young people's lives: These are just ______ examples of what many parents and the media ______ hip hop for. However, ______ the often negative image, it ______ be denied that hip hop is one of ______ musical genres in the whole world. Since its beginnings in the 1970s, hip hop ______ a global platform ______ brings together young people and ______ them a sense of identity. People from ______ different backgrounds share their love for the music, art and lifestyle of hip hop. It might be worth ______ about that as well before condemning a whole culture ______ (easy).

MEDIATION 25 Teenage slang → SB 87/1, S16

Your American friend Archer wants to know more about the German tradition of selecting the "teen slang word of the year". Read the three newspaper articles and write Archer an English e-mail (about 150 words) in which you tell him about the selection process and the different opinions on the idea of choosing a teen slang word of the year.

Über eine Million Jugendliche haben auch 2021 wieder das Jugendwort des Jahres gewählt. Bis August hatte ein auf Wörterbücher spezialisierter Verlag Vorschläge für das Jugendwort des Jahres gesammelt. Aus diesen Einsendungen wurden die Top 10 ausgewählt, über die dann in einem Online-Voting abgestimmt werden konnte. Dabei setzte sich „cringe" gegen Vorschläge wie „sus" oder „sheesh" durch. „Cringe" wird in Situationen verwendet, in denen einem etwas unangenehm oder peinlich ist. Das Jugendwort des Jahres stand immer wieder in der Kritik, vor allem da bis 2019 eine Jury aus Erwachsenen über das Jugendwort abgestimmt hatte.

Hanna Feste, Tageszeitung, 2021

Klar, das Jugendwort des Jahres ist eine PR-Aktion. Ebenso klar ist, dass vermutlich die wenigsten Jugendlichen tatsächlich so reden. Dennoch finde ich die Aktion gelungen. Den Gewinn hat allerdings weniger die Jugend, sondern eher die Eltern und Großeltern. Vor allem wenn die sich schon im Vorfeld die zur Auswahl stehenden Vorschläge zu Gemüte geführt haben. So erfahren sie immerhin, was angeblich beim Nachwuchs so alles abgeht, zumindest wortmäßig. Ganz nebenbei fühlt man sich bei diesem Schaulaufen an die eigene Jugendzeit erinnert. So kann man genüsslich den Nachwuchs mit Jugendwörtern aus vergangenen Zeiten traktieren und ihn raten lassen, was damit gemeint war, wenn man sich früher zusammen mit einem steilen Zahn zunächst ein Matsch am Paddel gönnte und danach dem Fummelbunker einen Besuch abstattete. Wie bitte? Ist doch klar: Dass man mit einem attraktiven Mädchen erst ein Eis am Stiel genossen hatte und dann in die Disko ging. Ob die Anbandelei tatsächlich so ablief, sei dahingestellt, genauso wie die Frage, ob die Wahl eines Jugendwortes sprachwissenschaftlich gesehen wirklich sinnvoll ist.

Klaus Zintz, Stuttgarter Nachrichten, 2017 (adaptiert)

Jedes Mal, wenn das „Jugendwort des Jahres" gewählt und verkündet wurde, dann sehen sich Jury und Verlag mit drei ewig gleichen kritischen Einwänden konfrontiert.

Der erste kommt von den universitären Linguisten und lautet, die ganze Veranstaltung sei wissenschaftlich anfechtbarer Unsinn. Der Vorwurf ist noch lauter geworden, seitdem die Linguistik immer mehr zu einer Computerwissenschaft wird, deren Vertreter sich mit großen elektronischen Textkorpora beschäftigen, aber immer weniger mit der unreinen Realität einer lebendigen Sprache: Literatur, Witze, Umgangssprache, Dialekt, Klosprüche, Gruppenjargons – also all jenen Bereiche, über die sich nur sehr schwer allgemeine Aussagen treffen lassen, die im nächsten Dorf und an der nächsten Klowand immer noch gültig sind.

Das zweite Standardargument lautet, das jeweilige „Jugendwort des Jahres" sei schon uralt. Dagegen kann man mit Blick auf die seit 500 Jahren fassbare Geschichte deutscher Jugendsprachen erwidern, dass ein Wort schon längst in der allgemeinen Umgangssprache angelangt sein kann und dennoch weiter von Jugendlichen gebraucht wird. Auch sind viele Wörter aus Jugendsprachen von gestern längst in den allgemeinen Wortschatz eingegangen. Pumpen mit der Bedeutung „leihen" ist ein Beispiel. Aber auch fast der gesamte Wortschatz der Sechzigerjahre-Gegenkultur: Dealer, Fixer etc.

Der dritte ewiggleiche Kritikpunkt geht so: „Das kennt doch keiner", „Wer sagt das denn?" Man will damit andeuten, dass eine weltfremde Jury sich für ein ungebräuchliches oder gar erfundenes Orchideenwort entschieden hat. Doch wer so argumentiert, verkennt, dass es nicht nur eine Jugendsprache gibt, sondern viele. Regionale Unterschiede sind zwar nicht mehr so ausgeprägt wie in den alten Zeiten, als es noch keine elektronischen Kommunikationskanäle gab. Aber dafür ist die Jugendkultur in definierte Grüppchen aufgesplittert.

Matthias Heine, Die Welt, 2021 (adaptiert)

SPEAKING **26** ## Influencers → SB 87/1, S14, S17

a) ***Warm-up:*** *Together with a partner, talk about what makes an influencer successful, the products and where they advertise, and why people become influencers.*

b) ***Monologue:*** *Describe the cartoon to your partner. Analyse the cartoon and comment on what the speaker in your cartoon believes about influencers.*

Partner A

Partner B

Think about it Dad: as a Social Media influencer, I could lobby gardeners around the world to plant more carrots...

c) ***Dialogue:*** *Together with your partner, explain what kinds of influencers you can see in the picture and discuss the pros and cons of their impact. Then comment on why influencers are popular and how they build relationships with their followers. Include the images, cartoons and useful phrases in your discussion.*

Useful phrases

Influencers are good / bad examples when … | They promote products / businesses which … | more / less healthy / social lifestyle | This can lead to … | trustworthy / authentic / artistic content | advertisement / marketing strategy | … has an impact on … | … can affect spending / mental health / body images / opinions | consumerism | to edit / retouch | to draw a lot of attention | to collaborate with | a large / small audience | a (reliable) recommendation / review | to build trust / relationships | to gain / lose followers

Self-assessment

On this page you can assess your performance. Look at the exercises in this workbook unit again and colour the traffic lights in the grid. Which skill(s) would you like to improve? The last column will tell you where to find help in your book.

Skill	Exercise(s)	Check	Help
LISTENING / VIEWING			
I know how to ...			
– understand the gist and the detail in listening texts and video clips (e.g. interview, talk, podcast, radio programme).	3, 8, 20, 22	○ ○ ○	S13
READING			
I know how to ...			
– understand and analyse a magazine article.	6 a)–c)	○ ○ ○	S5–6, S11
– understand and analyse a song.	10 a), c)–d)	○ ○ ○	S5–6
– understand and analyse an extract from a novel.	13 a), c)–f)	○ ○ ○	S5–6
– understand and analyse social media posts.	14 a)–b)	○ ○ ○	S3, S5–6, S17
– understand and analyse a poem.	19	○ ○ ○	S5–6, S14
SPEAKING			
I know how to ...			
– have a discussion with a partner.	2, 6 d), 10 e), 14 c), 26 a), c)	○ ○ ○	S14
– create and present a short video.	4	○ ○ ○	S15, S19
– give a short presentation.	21	○ ○ ○	S15
– describe and discuss a cartoon.	26 b)	○ ○ ○	S17
WRITING			
I know how to ...			
– analyse a movie trailer.	5	○ ○ ○	S8–10, S19
– write an argumentative essay.	12	○ ○ ○	S7–10
– write a diary entry.	13 g)	○ ○ ○	S7–9
– write a newspaper article.	13 g)	○ ○ ○	S7–10
MEDIATION			
I know how to ...			
– transfer relevant information into the target language in a way that is appropriate to the target audience and the situation.	9, 25	○ ○ ○	S5, S16
MEDIA COMPETENCE			
I know how to ...			
– use social media.	17, 18	○ ○ ○	S3
VOCABULARY / GRAMMAR			
I know how to ...			
– use relevant vocabulary and appropriate grammar to talk and write about youth and culture.	1, 7, 11, 13 b), 16, 23, 24	○ ○ ○	S1–2
– how to deal with unknown words.	10 b)	○ ○ ○	S1–2

SPEAKING

1 Showing support → SB 89/1

a) *Get together with a partner. Describe one of the cartoon characters each, then analyse the cartoon together.*

b) *Choose an issue you would protest against and create your own T-shirt slogan that demonstrates your position.*

VOCABULARY

2 Talking about music and protest → SB 89/2

a) *Use the following words to make useful phrases for the topics* ***protest*** *and* ***musical influences****. In your exercise book, write two lists. Add at least three more phrases to each list.*

abolition | to advocate | to be aimed | to be based | to be commercially | to demand | to express | to fight | to launch | musical | non-violent | to speak out | to spread | to take | to trace back	to the Black community | a campaign | elements from | against a common enemy | genre | around the globe | human rights | opposition | protest | against racism | structural change | successful | on a tune | at a young audience | of slavery

b) *Use some of the phrases from a) in their correct forms to complete the short wiki article on songs with social or political messages.*

Musical artists have written songs of various ____________________ about social issues in order to ____________________ or to ____________________ to politicians' abuse of power. Many bands ____________________ and earned millions of dollars with politically-motivated song texts. Music as a form of ____________________ can raise awareness, which in turn motivates individuals to ____________________ that aim to ____________________ ____________________ (e.g. a racist group, an unfair government). The music is usually not ____________________ alone, but at people of all ages who agree with the messages of the songs. Critical songs often ____________________ as their importance becomes recognised worldwide and they stay relevant for decades because social change is a rather slow process. One example of this is "Killing in the Name" by *Rage Against The Machine*, which ____________________ and police brutality. A more recent example of this is *Body Count*'s song "No Lives Matter" that ____________________ and anti-racism.

WRITING

c) *Are protest songs an effective way to bring about change? Write an argumentative essay (about 200 words).*

Final self-assessment

Using this grid, you can assess your overall performance during the school year. Note down what you're good at and what could be improved.

Skill / Knowledge gain		
READING		
– I know about the typical features of text types.	☐	☐
– I can get the gist of a written text quickly.	☐	☐
– I know how to analyse the main elements of a literary text (structure, narrative perspective, setting, characters, plot).	☐	☐
– I know how to analyse the main elements of a factual text (structure, line of arguments, language/style).	☐	☐
– I can identify stylistic devices in songs, poetry and speeches.	☐	☐
WRITING		
– I can plan and structure my text regarding my goal.	☐	☐
– I can write clear, understandable paragraphs and link them in a logical way.	☐	☐
– I'm good at inventing characters and stories.	☐	☐
– I use the language/register that is appropriate for my target group.	☐	☐
LISTENING / VIEWING		
– I can get the gist of a spoken text quickly.	☐	☐
– I'm good at listening for details.	☐	☐
– I'm good at analysing the atmosphere in a scene.	☐	☐
SPEAKING		
– I can speak fluently and have no difficulties pronouncing English sounds.	☐	☐
– I use fillers and feedback phrases to interact with other speakers.	☐	☐
– I'm good at presenting and explaining things.	☐	☐
– I know how to introduce arguments and link ideas in a discussion.	☐	☐
MEDIATION		
– I can identify quickly what is relevant regarding the situation and the person I mediate for.	☐	☐
– I'm good at paraphrasing what I can't translate exactly.	☐	☐
MEDIA COMPETENCE		
– I know where and how to find relevant information.	☐	☐
– I'm able to judge if a source is reliable.	☐	☐
SOCIAL SKILLS		
– I'm good at cooperating with others and giving them constructive feedback.	☐	☐
– I treat others respectfully and respect their privacy on social media.	☐	☐
BASIC KNOWLEDGE		
– I know enough vocabulary and grammar to present and discuss the texts and topics we have done in this school year.	☐	☐

If you need help with ideas for the skills you'd like to improve, talk to your teacher.

Irregular verbs

infinitive	simple past	past participle	German
be [bi:]	was [wɒz]/were [wɜ:]	been [bi:n]	sein
bear [beə]	bore [bɔ:]	borne / *AE:* born [bɔ:n]	tragen
beat [bi:t]	beat [bi:t]	beaten ['bi:tn] / *AE:* beat [bi:t]	schlagen
become [bɪ'kʌm]	became [bɪ'keɪm]	become [bɪ'kʌm]	werden
begin [bɪ'gɪn]	began [bɪ'gæn]	begun [bɪ'gʌn]	beginnen, anfangen
bend [bend]	bent [bent]	bent [bent]	biegen, beugen
bet [bet]	bet [bet]/betted ['betɪd]	bet [bet]/betted ['betɪd]	wetten
bite [baɪt]	bit [bɪt]	bitten ['bɪtn]	beißen
blow [bləʊ]	blew [blu:]	blown [bləʊn]	blasen, pusten
break [breɪk]	broke [brəʊk]	broken ['brəʊkn]	(zer-)brechen, kaputt machen
breed [bri:d]	bred [bred]	bred [bred]	züchten, sich vermehren
bring [brɪŋ]	brought [brɔ:t]	brought [brɔ:t]	(mit-)bringen
build [bɪld]	built [bɪlt]	built [bɪlt]	bauen
burn [bɜ:n]	burnt [bɜ:nt]/burned [bɜ:nd]	burnt [bɜ:nt]/burned [bɜ:nd]	brennen
burst [bɜ:st]	burst [bɜ:st]/bursted ['bɜ:stɪd]	burst [bɜ:st]/bursted ['bɜ:stɪd]	bersten, platzen
buy [baɪ]	bought [bɔ:t]	bought [bɔ:t]	kaufen
cast [kɑ:st]	cast [kɑ:st]	cast [kɑ:st]	werfen
catch [kætʃ]	caught [kɔ:t]	caught [kɔ:t]	fangen
choose [tʃu:z]	chose [tʃəʊz]	chosen ['tʃəʊzn]	(aus-)wählen
come [kʌm]	came [keɪm]	come [kʌm]	kommen
cost [kɒst]	cost [kɒst]	cost [kɒst]	kosten
cling [klɪŋ]	clang [klæŋ]	clung [klʌŋ]	kleben, klammern
creep [kri:p]	crept [krept]	crept [krept]	schleichen
cut [kʌt]	cut [kʌt]	cut [kʌt]	schneiden
deal [di:l]	dealt [delt]	dealt [delt]	(be-)handeln
dig [dɪg]	dug [dʌg]	dug [dʌg]	graben
do [du:]	did [dɪd]	done [dʌn]	machen, tun
draw [drɔ:]	drew [dru:]	drawn [drɔ:n]	zeichnen, ziehen
dream [dri:m]	dreamt [dremt]/dreamed [dri:md]	dreamt [dremt]/dreamed [dri:md]	träumen
drink [drɪŋk]	drank [dræŋk]	drunk [drʌŋk]	trinken
drive [draɪv]	drove [drəʊv]	driven ['drɪvn]	fahren, treiben
eat [i:t]	ate [et/eɪt]	eaten ['i:tn]	essen
fall [fɔ:l]	fell [fel]	fallen ['fɔ:lən]	fallen
feed [fi:d]	fed [fed]	fed [fed]	füttern, ernähren
feel [fi:l]	felt [felt]	felt [felt]	fühlen
fight [faɪt]	fought [fɔ:t]	fought [fɔ:t]	kämpfen, (sich) streiten
find [faɪnd]	found [faʊnd]	found [faʊnd]	finden
fit [fɪt]	fit [fɪt]/fitted ['fɪtɪd]	fit [fɪt]/fitted ['fɪtɪd]	passen
fly [flaɪ]	flew [flu:]	flown [fləʊn]	fliegen
forbid [fə'bɪd]	forbade [fə'bæd]	forbidden [fə'bɪdn]	verbieten
forget [fə'get]	forgot [fə'gɒt]	forgotten [fə'gɒtn]	vergessen
forgive [fə'gɪv]	forgave [fə'geɪv]	forgiven [fə'gɪvn]	vergeben, verzeihen
freeze [fri:z]	froze [frəʊz]	frozen ['frəʊzn]	gefrieren, erstarren
get [get]	got [gɒt]	got [gɒt]/*AE:* gotten ['gɒtn]	bekommen, erhalten
give [gɪv]	gave [geɪv]	given ['gɪvn]	geben
go [gəʊ]	went [went]	gone [gɒn]	gehen, fahren
grow [grəʊ]	grew [gru:]	grown [grəʊn]	wachsen, anbauen, züchten
hang [hæŋ]	hung [hʌŋ]	hung [hʌŋ]	hängen
have [hæv]	had [hæd]	had [hæd]	haben
hear [hɪə]	heard [hɜ:d]	heard [hɜ:d]	hören
hide [haɪd]	hid [hɪd]	hidden ['hɪdn]	(sich) verstecken
hit [hɪt]	hit [hɪt]	hit [hɪt]	schlagen, treffen
hold [həʊld]	held [held]	held [held]	halten
hurt [hɜ:t]	hurt [hɜ:t]	hurt [hɜ:t]	verletzen, sich weh tun
keep [ki:p]	kept [kept]	kept [kept]	(auf-)bewahren, behalten
know [nəʊ]	knew [nju:]	known [nəʊn]	kennen, wissen
lay [leɪ]	laid [leɪd]	laid [leɪd]	legen
lead [li:d]	led [led]	led [led]	führen
lean [li:n]	leant [lent]/leaned [li:nd]	leant [lent]/leaned [li:nd]	lehnen, beugen
leap [li:p]	leapt [lept]/leaped [li:pt]	leapt [lept]/leaped [li:pt]	springen
learn [lɜ:n]	learnt [lɜ:nt]/learned [lɜ:nd]	learnt [lɜ:nt]/learned [lɜ:nd]	lernen
leave [li:v]	left [left]	left [left]	(ver-)lassen

infinitive	simple past	past participle	German
lend [lend]	lent [lent]	lent [lent]	leihen
let [let]	let [let]	let [let]	lassen
lie [laɪ]	lay [leɪ]	lain [leɪn]	liegen
lose [lu:z]	lost [lɒst]	lost [lɒst]	verlieren
make [meɪk]	made [meɪd]	made [meɪd]	machen, tun
mean [mi:n]	meant [ment]	meant [ment]	bedeuten, meinen
meet [mi:t]	met [met]	met [met]	treffen
pay [peɪ]	paid [peɪd]	paid [peɪd]	(be-)zahlen
put [pʊt]	put [pʊt]	put [pʊt]	legen, setzen, stellen
read [ri:d]	read [red]	read [red]	lesen
ride [raɪd]	rode [rəʊd]	ridden ['rɪdn]	fahren, reiten
ring [rɪŋ]	rang [ræŋ]	rung [rʌŋ]	klingeln, läuten
rise [raɪz]	rose [rəʊz]	risen ['rɪzn]	aufsteigen, sich erheben
run [rʌn]	ran [ræn]	run [rʌn]	laufen, rennen
say [seɪ]	said [sed]	said [sed]	sagen
see [si:]	saw [sɔ:]	seen [si:n]	sehen
seek [si:k]	sought [sɔ:t]	sought [sɔ:t]	suchen
sell [sel]	sold [səʊld]	sold [səʊld]	verkaufen
send [send]	sent [sent]	sent [sent]	senden, verschicken
set [set]	set [set]	set [set]	setzen, einrichten
sew [səʊ]	sewed [səʊd]	sewn [səʊn]/sewed [səʊd]	nähen
shake [ʃeɪk]	shook [ʃʊk]	shaken ['ʃeɪkn]	schütteln
shine [ʃaɪn]	shone [ʃɒn]	shone [ʃɒn]	scheinen
shoot [ʃu:t]	shot [ʃɒt]	shot [ʃɒt]	schießen
show [ʃəʊ]	showed [ʃəʊd]	shown [ʃəʊn]	zeigen
shrink [ʃrɪŋk]	shrank [ʃræŋk]	shrunk [ʃrʌŋk]	schrumpfen, weichen
sing [sɪŋ]	sang [sæŋ]	sung [sʌŋ]	singen
sink [sɪŋk]	sank [sæŋk]	sunk [sʌŋk]	sinken
sit [sɪt]	sat [sæt]	sat [sæt]	sitzen
sleep [sli:p]	slept [slept]	slept [slept]	schlafen
slide [slaɪd]	slid [slɪd]	slid [slɪd]	rutschen
smell [smel]	smelt [smelt]/smelled [smeld]	smelt [smelt]/smelled [smeld]	riechen, duften
sow [səʊ]	sowed [səʊd]	sown [səʊn]/sowed [səʊd]	säen
speak [spi:k]	spoke [spəʊk]	spoken ['spəʊkn]	sprechen
speed [spi:d]	sped [sped]/speeded ['spi:dɪd]	sped [sped]/speeded ['spi:dɪd]	sausen, rasen
spell [spel]	spelt [spelt]/spelled [speld]	spelt [spelt]/spelled [speld]	buchstabieren
spend [spend]	spent [spent]	spent [spent]	ausgeben, verbringen
spin [spɪn]	span [spæn]/spun [spʌn]	spun [spʌn]	drehen, spinnen
spit [spɪt]	spat [spæt]	spat [spæt]	spucken
split [splɪt]	split [splɪt]	split [splɪt]	spalten, teilen
spread [spred]	spread [spred]	spread [spred]	(sich) verbreiten
stand [stænd]	stood [stʊd]	stood [stʊd]	stehen
steal [sti:l]	stole [stəʊl]	stolen ['stəʊlən]	stehlen
stick [stɪk]	stuck [stʌk]	stuck [stʌk]	kleben, stecken
sting [stɪŋ]	stung [stʌŋ]	stung [stʌŋ]	stechen
strike [straɪk]	struck [strʌk]	struck [strʌk]	schlagen, zuschlagen
strive [straɪv]	strove [strəʊv]/strived [straɪvd]	striven [strɪvn]/strived [straɪvd]	streben, sich bemühen
swear [sweə]	swore [swɔ:]	sworn [swɔ:n]	schwören, fluchen
sweep [swi:p]	swept [swept]	swept [swept]	fegen
swell [swel]	swelled [sweld]	swollen ['swəʊlən]/swelled [sweld]	anschwellen, anwachsen
swim [swɪm]	swam [swæm]	swum [swʌm]	schwimmen
swing [swɪŋ]	swung [swʌŋ]	swung [swʌŋ]	schwingen
take [teɪk]	took [tʊk]	taken ['teɪkn]	nehmen
teach [ti:tʃ]	taught [tɔ:t]	taught [tɔ:t]	unterrichten, lehren, beibringen
tell [tel]	told [təʊld]	told [təʊld]	erzählen
think [θɪŋk]	thought [θɔ:t]	thought [θɔ:t]	(nach-)denken, glauben
throw [θrəʊ]	threw [θru:]	thrown [θrəʊn]	werfen
understand [ˌʌndə'stænd]	understood [ˌʌndə'stʊd]	understood [ˌʌndə'stʊd]	verstehen
upset [ʌp'set]	upset [ʌp'set]	upset [ʌp'set]	aufregen
wake [weɪk]	woke [wəʊk]	woken ['wəʊkn]	wecken, aufwachen
wear [weə]	wore [wɔ:]	worn [wɔ:n]	anhaben, tragen
weep [wi:p]	wept [wept]	wept [wept]	weinen
win [wɪn]	won [wʌn]	won [wʌn]	gewinnen, siegen
write [raɪt]	wrote [rəʊt]	written ['rɪtn]	schreiben